11/19   **DATE DUE**

FEB 07 2020

MAR 09 2020

DEC 2 0 2021

mu   als

mug meals

more than 100 no-fuss ways to make a delicious microwave meal in minutes

Leslie Bilderback

PHOTOGRAPHS BY TERI LYN FISHER

ST. MARTIN'S GRIFFIN
NEW YORK

This book is for everyone, but especially college students.
When I wrote it I had two children living in college dorms.
I saw the contents of those tiny refrigerators,
and I think it's high time y'all learn how to cook more than cereal
and Cup O' Noodles. You'll thank me later.

www.stmartins.com

Book design by Rita Sowins / Sowins Design

The Library of Congress Cataloging-in-Publication Data is available upon request.

ISBN 978-1-250-06720-3 (trade paperback)
ISBN 978-1-4668-7521-0 (e-book)

St. Martin's Griffin books may be purchased for educational, business, or promotional use. For information on bulk purchases, please contact the Macmillan Corporate and Premium Sales Department at 1-800-221-7945, extension 5442, or write to specialmarkets@macmillan.com.

First Edition: September 2015

10 9 8 7 6 5 4 3 2 1

contents

introduction

Welcome to Mug Meals! You are about to embark on a culinary voyage of discovery. That appliance you thought was only for reheating the morning's coffee actually can cook real food. Not store-bought frozen dinners. Not last night's doggy bag, but real food, made from fresh ingredients. You will soon find your kitchen filled with good food that tastes great and is good for you. Did I just blow your mind?

These recipes have been developed with several kinds of cooks in mind:

- For the cook with limited equipment—college students, hotel residents, motor home travelers—these recipes provide satisfying, whole-food meals that are completely microwaveable. The majority of these recipes use only a knife, a mug, and a fork.

- For busy people with a packed schedule, these recipes are, for the most part, finished in 5 to 10 minutes.

- For kids who are not ready to use the stove, the microwave offers real cooking without scary flames. Because it is real cooking, and not merely reheating, it teaches real cooking techniques. But because the mugs do get hot, it helps to teach caution during the preparation of foods. These recipes are a nice prerequisite to using the real stove.

- For people focusing on portion size, these mug-size meals emphasize flavor over quantity, and demonstrate just how satisfying a standard portion can be.

This is not merely fast food. If all you are concerned about is speed, you could buy a frozen dinner for the microwave and zap it. These recipes are real cooking in small amounts. Yes, it's quick, but the time saved is not correlated to poor nutrition or loss of flavor.

Mug Meals Tips and Tricks

• Ingredients and Measurements •

Recipe books are very useful (says the cookbook author), but they are by no means iron-clad. While specific measurements of things like chopped vegetables, herbs, and seasonings are given in the recipes here, cooks should feel empowered to "eyeball" it. There are few cases where slight variations will make any difference in the finished product. So if you like your food "herbier" or "veggi-er" or meatier, or saltier, then you should make it that way.

Part of the benefit of mug cooking is convenience. This makes it the perfect vehicle for leftovers and precooked foods. In this age of extreme food waste, it's nice to have a cache of recipes that facilitate leftover use. In this spirit, if you don't have a specific ingredient on hand, I have provided lots of options for substitutions. The same is true for spices, herbs, and various condiments. If you don't have a specific ingredient on hand, don't make a special trip to the store. Use what you have. After all, necessity breeds creativity.

• Mugs •

These mug recipes were designed to be made in mugs. But here's a secret—they do not have to be cooked in mugs. Any microwave-safe vessel that fits in your microwave will work. Feel free to cook in a bowl, or a glass loaf pan, or a recycled Cool Whip container. It's all good!

Large and jumbo mugs are generally the container of choice for these recipes. This refers to vessels sometimes called cappuccino mugs, soup mugs or souvenir mugs. When the recipe calls for a large mug, it should have a capacity of at least 12 to 14 ounces (1½ to 1¾ cups). A jumbo mug should hold at least 16 to 20 ounces (2 to 2½ cups). The size is usually specified so that the contents will not boil up and over, messing up your microwave.

● Microwaves ●

Just as there are no standard mug sizes, there are no standard microwave ovens. Some offer various settings, while others have only an on and off setting. But they all work the same way. The microwave radiation is absorbed by water in the food, setting the molecules into motion. But the various microwave oven models and settings cook at different rates. For this reason, cooking times in this book are given in a range. Always start with the shorter time first. Then check your mug meal, and continue cooking if necessary in 10- to 15-second increments. After a couple mug meals you will understand how long it takes your microwave to cook.

One more thing about microwave ovens—they do not get much hotter than the temperature of boiling water, which is 212°F. This means that foods do not brown much. This is most noticeable in microwave baking, and when you microwave meats. Some of these items will not look like the foods that come out of your standard oven or are cooked on your stovetop. Don't let that put you off. They taste great, and serve the purpose here, which is widening your microwave repertoire. These recipes are not something you'll see referenced in the *Zagat Guide*, but they will enable you to eat a fresh, homemade meal with limited resources.

● Thinking Ahead ●

Several recipes call for ingredients that need to be precooked. There are directions for microwaving single portions in a mug, but consider cooking larger batches. If pasta, grains, meat, poultry, and seafood are cooked ahead and stored in single portions, whipping up a mug meal is even quicker. Ziplock bags of cooked pasta, grains, and meats are easily frozen for several weeks.

● Cleanup ●

Much of the time saved by microwaving mug meals is in the cleanup. No large pots, pans, or skillets to scour. No multiple tools and gadgets to clean. No greasy, splattered stovetops to wipe down. However, the mugs will get dirty in a big way. Especially when prolonged cooking is involved, the mugs get caked with cooked foods. The best, and easiest, way to clean this mess up is to soak them. Fill the mugs completely to the rim with water and set aside. After a good soaking, use a brush to scrub out the residue. Don't leave it up to the dishwashing machine. Even if your dishwasher is a superdeluxe model, it will not be able to scrub out food cooked on by a microwave.

● Finally ●

Use these recipes as a jumping-off point. Once you come to terms with the ease of microwave cooking in small batches, the possibilities are endless. Be creative! Have fun! Get healthy!

You can also use the methods you learn here to help in your regular cooking. Quick- cooking vegetables, sauces, and proteins can speed up prep for larger meals cooked on a standard stove. Next time you tackle a big dinner party, put some mug meal technology to use.

Now, get cooking!

1

breakfast baking

It is no accident that these recipes bear an uncanny resemblance to mug cakes. If you have experienced the wonder of mug cakes, you'll be a master at the recipes in this chapter. If you are unfamiliar with mug "microwavery," these recipes are a great place to start.

Cinnamon Roll

The greatest day of my life was the day I figured out how to bake yeast dough in the microwave. OK, it falls just behind my children being born and the day I was married, but only just.

INGREDIENTS

½ cup warm water

½ teaspoon granulated yeast

1 tablespoon brown sugar

¼ cup golden raisins

6 tablespoons bread or all-purpose flour

Pinch of kosher salt

1 teaspoon ground cinnamon

¼ cup confectioners' sugar

1 tablespoon whole milk

¼ cup pecan pieces

METHOD

1. In a jumbo mug, combine the water, yeast, brown sugar, and raisins. Mix together well, then set aside to proof for 15 minutes. When the yeast is bubbly, stir in the flour, salt, and ½ teaspoon of the cinnamon. Mix vigorously with a fork to create an elastic dough. Cover the mug with a damp paper towel and set aside to rise for 30 to 60 minutes.

2. Microwave the dough for 1½ to 2½ minutes until risen and firm, but not dry. In a separate mug, mix the remaining ½ teaspoon cinnamon with the confectioners' sugar and the milk until well combined. Drizzle over the finished cinnamon roll, and sprinkle with the pecan pieces. Serve immediately.

Banana Bread

This is a go-to recipe for beginning bakers because it is very hard to mess up. The one indispensible element is the overripe banana. Don't try it with beautiful, perfectly ripe, yellow specimens; they won't be sweet enough. It's the mushy black ones that make the best bread.

INGREDIENTS

½ overripe banana

1 large egg

1 tablespoon vegetable oil

2 tablespoons sour cream

½ teaspoon pure vanilla extract

¼ cup packed brown sugar

1 tablespoon chopped walnuts

½ cup self-rising flour (or ½ cup all-purpose flour and ¼ teaspoon baking powder)

Pinch of ground cinnamon

Pinch of freshly grated nutmeg

Pinch of kosher salt

Unsalted butter or cream cheese, for serving

METHOD

1. Put the banana in a mug and mash it well with a fork. Add the egg and oil and whisk it together well. Stir in the sour cream, vanilla, sugar, and nuts. Add the flour, spices, and salt. Beat the batter until smooth

2. Divide the batter between two mugs and microwave separately for 1½ to 2½ minutes each until risen and firm. Serve immediately topped with a pat of butter or a schmear of cream cheese

> ### • VARIATIONS •
>
> **FRUITY:** Add a variety of dried fruits, such as dark or golden raisins, cranberries, cherries, figs, or dates. Soak ¼ cup of the dried fruits in hot water for 15 to 30 minutes, or overnight if you think that far in advance. Then drain them and fold into the batter with the nuts.
>
> **TROPICAL:** Make this recipe a little more exotic with the addition of coconut, macadamia nuts, and dried tropical fruits like dehydrated pineapple, mango, or banana chips. Use about ¼ cup of these elements in place of the walnuts.

Lemon-Poppy Seed Muffins

MAKES 2 MUGS

Wake up your taste buds with the sweet tang of this popular morning muffin.

INGREDIENTS

2 tablespoons unsalted butter

Finely grated zest of 1 lemon

1 large egg

2 tablespoons buttermilk

1 teaspoon poppy seeds

1 teaspoon pure vanilla extract

¼ cup granulated sugar

6 tablespoons self-rising flour (or 6 tablespoons all-purpose flour plus ⅛ teaspoon baking powder)

Pinch of kosher salt

¼ cup confectioners' sugar

1 tablespoon whole milk

METHOD

1. Put the butter and lemon zest in a mug and microwave for 30 to 60 seconds until the butter has melted. Whisk in the egg with a fork. Stir in the buttermilk, poppy seeds, vanilla, and granulated sugar. Add the flour and salt and beat the batter with a fork until smooth.

2. Divide the batter between two mugs. Microwave separately for 1½ to 2½ minutes each until risen and firm.

3. In a separate mug, beat together the confectioners' sugar and milk until smooth. Pour over the finished muffins, and serve.

Blueberry Muffins

These muffins are an essential element in any breakfast repertoire. Fresh, sweet, height-of-the-season berries are ideal, but they are only available for a limited time. For the rest of the year, frozen berries will work just fine. Zap them in a little water for 30 seconds just to take off the chill before you add them to your mug batter.

INGREDIENTS

2 tablespoons unsalted butter

Finely grated zest of ½ lemon

1 large egg

¼ cup granulated sugar

3 tablespoons buttermilk

½ teaspoon pure vanilla extract

6 tablespoons self-rising flour (or 6 tablespoons all-purpose flour plus ¼ teaspoon baking powder)

Pinch of kosher salt

¼ cup blueberries (or try it with other fresh berries, diced stone fruits, or dried fruits)

Confectioners' sugar or marmalade, for serving

METHOD

1. Put the butter and lemon zest in a large mug and microwave for 30 to 60 seconds until melted. Whisk in the egg with a fork. Stir in the granulated sugar, buttermilk, and vanilla. Add the flour and salt and combine. Fold in the blueberries. Divide the batter between two mugs. (You can top them with a sprinkle of cinnamon sugar or streusel if you'd like. See Coffee Cake recipe, page 15). Microwave separately for 1½ to 2½ minutes each until risen and firm. Serve immediately, topped with a dusting of confectioners' sugar or a spoonful of marmalade.

> ### • VARIATIONS •
>
> **CINNAMON-SUGAR:** A teaspoon of cinnamon-sugar on top of the batter before cooking makes a lovely topping. Use 1 part cinnamon to 3 parts granulated sugar.
>
> **FRUIT OPTIONS:** This recipe can also be made with raspberries, blackberries, huckleberries, cranberries, diced stone fruits, tropical fruits, and dried fruits.

Oat and Seed Muffins

MAKES 2 MUGS

Seeds are superhealthy! Flaxseeds, especially, are the latest wonder food, benefitting you with added fiber, healthy omega-3 fatty acids, and reducing the risks of heart disease and cancer—plus, the seeds add a delicious, nutty crunch. Yes, this recipe has sugar, which might negate the seed benefits, but we'll just let that slide.

INGREDIENTS

3 tablespoons raisins

2 tablespoons apple juice

½ teaspoon pure vanilla extract

1 large egg

3 tablespoons whole milk

¼ cup packed brown sugar

¼ cup self-rising flour (or ¼ cup all-purpose flour plus ⅛ teaspoon baking powder)

2 tablespoons old-fashioned rolled oats (not steel cut)

1 tablespoon flaxseeds

1 tablespoon sunflower seeds

1 teaspoon sesame seeds

Pinch of ground cinnamon

Pinch of kosher salt

¼ cup streusel (See Coffee Cake recipe, page 15)

METHOD

1. In a large mug, combine the raisins, apple juice, and vanilla. Microwave for 30 to 60 seconds, then set aside for 5 to 10 minutes to allow the raisins to plump while you make the batter.

2. In a second mug, whisk the egg with a fork. Stir in the milk and brown sugar. Add the flour, oats, flaxseeds, sunflower seeds, sesame seeds, cinnamon, and salt and beat the batter until smooth. Fold in the plumped raisins and the soaking liquid.

3. Divide the batter between two mugs, and top each with the streusel. Microwave separately for 1½ to 2½ minutes each until risen and firm.

Corncake

Though usually cooked on the griddle, this recipe translates nicely to the microwave. It calls for corn flour, which is nothing more than finely ground cornmeal. If you have trouble locating it, you can substitute all-purpose flour, or grind cornmeal in a food processor or coffee mill until it is a fine powder.

INGREDIENTS

2 tablespoons unsalted butter

1 tablespoon chopped scallion

½ small jalapeño chile, diced (optional)

½ cup whole milk

1 large egg, separated

¼ cup corn flour (see headnote) or all-purpose flour

¼ cup cornmeal

½ teaspoon sugar

¼ teaspoon kosher salt

¼ cup corn kernels, fresh, frozen, or drained canned

METHOD

1. Put the butter, scallion, and diced jalapeño, if using, in a large mug and microwave for 20 to 30 seconds until the butter has melted. Add the milk and egg yolk and whisk in with a fork. Stir in the corn flour, cornmeal, sugar, and salt. Fold in the corn kernels.

2. In a separate mug, whisk the egg white using a battery-operated milk foamer (or do it the old-fashioned way, in a separate small bowl with a whisk). Fold the whipped white into the batter, then divide the batter between two mugs. Microwave separately for 1½ to 2½ minutes each until risen and firm.

Pumpkin Muffins

Pumpkin puree is easily made by zapping diced squash in water until tender, 3 to 4 minutes, then draining and mashing. Of course, you can buy pumpkin puree, both in large cans (in the canned fruit aisle) and in tiny jars (in the baby food aisle . . . shhh . . .it'll be our secret.)

INGREDIENTS

1 large egg

¼ cup pumpkin puree

2 tablespoons whole milk

¼ teaspoon pure vanilla extract

¼ cup packed brown sugar

¼ cup chopped pecan pieces

7 tablespoons (¼ cup plus 3 tablespoons) self-rising flour (or use all-purpose flour plus ¼ teaspoon baking powder)

Pinch of kosher salt

½ teaspoon pumpkin pie spice (⅛ teaspoon each of cinnamon, nutmeg, ginger, and a tiny pinch of ground cloves)

METHOD

1. In a large mug, whisk together the egg and pumpkin puree with a fork. Stir in the milk, vanilla, sugar, and pecans. Add the flour, salt, and pumpkin pie spice and beat the batter until smooth.

2. Divide the batter between two mugs. Microwave separately for 1½ to 2½ minutes each until risen and firm.

Coffee Cake

When I figured out coffee cake didn't actually have coffee in it, I was mighty disappointed. Serving it in a coffee mug, though, has lessened the pain.

INGREDIENTS

Streusel Topping

1 teaspoon granulated sugar

2 teaspoons whole wheat flour

1 teaspoon unsalted butter

Cake Batter

1 large egg

2 tablespoons vegetable oil

2 tablespoons buttermilk

¼ teaspoon pure vanilla extract

¼ cup packed brown sugar

6 tablespoons self-rising flour (or 6 tablespoons all-purpose flour plus ¼ teaspoons baking powder)

Pinch of kosher salt

METHOD

1. *To make the streusel topping:* In a large mug, combine the granulated sugar and whole wheat flour. Add the chilled butter, and cut it in, using a fork, until the mixture resembles coarse crumbs. Set aside in the refrigerator.

2. *To make the cake:* In a separate large mug, whisk together the egg, oil, and buttermilk. Stir in the vanilla and brown sugar, then add the self-rising flour and salt. Divide the batter between two mugs. Top each with half of the chilled streusel and microwave separately for 1½ to 2½ minutes each until risen and firm.

• VARIATIONS •

ADD-INS: Personalize this recipe with the addition of ½ cup of your favorite nuts, dried fruits, berries, or chocolate chips. Fold them into the batter just before you add the flour.

OATY-NUTTY STREUSEL: Enhance your streusel with the addition of 1 tablespoon of rolled oats, chopped nuts, and even some spice; try ground cinnamon, nutmeg, ginger and/or cardamom.

Buttermilk Pancakes

Yes, I know pancakes, by definition, should be cooked in a pan—or better yet, on a griddle. But this is the next best thing. Just close your eyes as you eat it, and imagine a lumberjack stack.

INGREDIENTS

2 tablespoons unsalted butter, plus a pat

1 tablespoon sugar

¾ cup buttermilk

1 large egg

½ cup all-purpose flour

½ teaspoon baking powder

Pinch of kosher salt

Maple syrup, for drizzling

METHOD

1. Put the 2 tablespoons of butter and the sugar in a large mug and microwave for 1 to 2 minutes until the butter has melted. Add the buttermilk and egg and whisk with a fork. Stir in the flour, baking powder, and salt.

2. Divide the batter between two mugs. Microwave separately for 1½ to 2½ minutes each until risen and firm. Serve immediately topped with the pat of butter and a drizzle of maple syrup.

> ### • VARIATIONS •
>
> **BUTTERMILK OPTIONS:** This recipe works just as well with a variety of dairy products. You can use regular milk, or keep the tang by using sour cream or plain yogurt.
>
> **PANCAKE GARNISH:** You can fold in 2–4 tablespoons of your favorite pancake embellishments, including chocolate chips or blueberries. You can also go the way of health by folding in oats and sunflower seeds.

Whole Wheat Banana-Nut Pancakes

Here is another recipe boosted from the griddle. They will never be as good as a griddle cake, but they will get you through your midweek pancake craving. You have that, too, right?

INGREDIENTS

2 teaspoons unsalted butter, plus a pat

1 tablespoon brown sugar

¾ cup whole milk

1 large egg

¼ cup pecan pieces

½ cup whole wheat flour

½ teaspoon baking powder

¼ teaspoon ground cinnamon

Pinch of kosher salt

½ ripe banana, sliced into rounds

Maple syrup, for serving

METHOD

1. Put the 2 teaspoons of butter in a large mug and micro-wave for 20 to 30 seconds until melted. Add the sugar, milk, and egg and whisk with a fork. Add the pecan pieces. Stir in the flour, baking powder, cinnamon, and salt. Fold in the sliced banana.

2. Divide the batter between two mugs. Microwave separately for 1½ to 2½ minutes each until risen and firm. Serve immediately with the pat of butter and maple syrup.

• VARIATIONS •

APPLE-CINNAMON: Cook one small, peeled, cored, and diced apple in the mug with the butter and ¼ teaspoon cinnamon for 1 to 2 minutes until tender. Then use the apples instead of the bananas.

BLUEBERRY: Add ¼ cup blueberries in place of, or in addition to, the pecans.

CHOCOLATE CHIP: Add ¼ cup chocolate chips in place of, or in addition to, the pecans.

Mug French Toast

You can divide this into two mugs if you're sharing, but mix it first in the jumbo mug for best results. But let's not kid ourselves—finishing off a jumbo mug of this French toast is no problem for true French toast connoisseurs.

INGREDIENTS

1 tablespoon unsalted butter

1 to 2 slices French bread, cubed (or use any bread you have on hand)

1 large egg

¼ cup whole milk

2 teaspoons sugar

⅛ teaspoon pure vanilla extract

¼ teaspoon ground cinnamon

Pinch of kosher salt

Maple syrup, for serving

METHOD

1. Put the butter in a jumbo mug and microwave it for 20 to 30 seconds until melted. Add the cubed bread and set aside.

2. In a separate mug, whisk together the egg, milk, sugar, vanilla, cinnamon, and salt. Pour the mixture over the cubed bread and let it sit for a minute or two, squishing the bread down so that it all gets saturated with the custard. Microwave for 1½ to 2½ minutes until risen and the egg is no longer runny. Top with maple syrup and serve immediately.

> • VARIATIONS •
>
> **EMBELLISHMENTS:** Add ¼ cup of your favorite garnish with the bread. Try it with fresh berries, dried fruits, chopped nuts, or chocolate chips.

Currant Scones

This recipe is a classic tea-time standard served at all the fancy teahouses. But who needs a teahouse when you have a mug and a microwave? Both the tea and the scone can be ready in minutes. Jolly good!

INGREDIENTS

¼ cup dried currants

½ cup water

½ cup self-rising flour (or use all-purpose flour plus ¼ teaspoon baking powder)

2 tablespoons sugar, plus extra for dusting

Pinch of kosher salt

1 tablespoon unsalted butter

3 tablespoons heavy cream (half-and-half or whole milk will work, too)

¼ teaspoon pure vanilla extract

Lemon curd, jam, or clotted cream, for serving

METHOD

1. In a small mug, combine the currants and water and microwave for 30 seconds. Set aside to plump while you make the rest of your scone.

2. In a jumbo mug, stir together the flour, sugar, and salt. Add the butter and cut it in using a fork, until the mixture resembles a coarse crumbs. Add the cream, vanilla, and drained plumped currants and stir just until combined. Dust the top with a pinch of granulated sugar, then microwave for 1 to 2 minutes until risen and firm. Serve immediately with lemon curd, jam, or clotted cream.

• VARIATIONS •

GARNISH GALORE: Create dozens of variations by simply replacing the currants with an equal portion of berries, nuts, chocolate chips, dried fruit, or chopped seasonal fruits.

SPICE IT UP: Add a teaspoon of grated citrus zest, or a ½ teaspoon of your favorite spices.

SAVORY: Omit the currants and vanilla, reduce the sugar to ½ teaspoon, then add ¼ cup of grated cheese, diced ham, crumbled bacon, caramelized onions, herbs, or mushrooms.

Toasty Oat Buttermilk Granola

Warm granola is the bomb on a cold winter morning. The buttermilk cuts the sweetness of most granolas, but you can use regular milk, too. And the berries make it almost healthy.

INGREDIENTS

1 teaspoon unsalted butter

½ cup granola

½ cup buttermilk (sour cream works, too)

Fresh berries, other seasonal fruit, or plumped raisins, for serving

METHOD

Melt the butter in a large mug in the microwave for 30 to 60 seconds. Add the granola and toss together. Stir in the buttermilk and microwave for another minute. Set aside for 5 minutes to cool slightly and allow the granola to absorb the liquid. Serve topped with fresh berries, other seasonal fruit, or plumped raisins.

Apple-Cinnamon Oatmeal

MAKES 2 MUGS

Microwaved oatmeal may not be a revelation to everyone, but it is worth mentioning here if for no other reason than it saves you from having to wash a crusty, pasty oatmeal pot.

INGREDIENTS

½ Fuji apple, cored and diced or grated

1 tablespoon brown sugar

1 tablespoon unsalted butter

¼ teaspoon ground cinnamon

¼ cup old fashioned rolled oats

½ cup whole milk

METHOD

In a jumbo mug, combine the sugar and apple. Toss together, top with the butter, and microwave for 30 to 60 seconds until the butter and sugar have liquefied. Stir in the oats and milk and microwave for another 1½ to 2½ minutes each, or until you reach your preferred oatmeal texture.

mug eggs anytime

Cooking eggs in the microwave is the secret to a quick and hearty breakfast. But don't reserve them just for breakfast. The beauty of the egg is its versatility. There are few microwavable foods that are as quick and easy.

Poached Eggs and Breakfast Hash

MAKES 1 MUG

This is the ideal meal to use up leftover meat and potatoes. But if you are out of leftovers, don't despair—cooking potatoes in the microwave is easy-peasy.

INGREDIENTS

1 slice bacon, diced

1 tablespoon chopped scallion

½ cup leftover cooked and diced white potato, sweet potato, or other cooked root vegetable

½ cup cooked meat, diced (ham, roast beef, corned beef, salami, sausage, or other cured meat)

Kosher salt

Freshly ground black pepper

1 large egg

METHOD

1. Combine the bacon and scallion in a large mug. Microwave for 1 to 2 minutes, stirring intermittently, until the bacon is crispy and the fat has rendered. Pour off all but 1 tablespoon of the fat. Add the potatoes and the meat and season with salt and pepper to taste. Microwave another minute, in the same manner, until the potatoes are warmed through.

2. Remove the mug from the microwave. Press a small indentation in the top of the hash. Add a teaspoon of water to the indentation, then crack in an egg, being careful not to break the yolk. Sprinkle a little water on top of the egg, then microwave for another 30 to 60 seconds, or until the egg white is firm but the yolk is still runny (or cook to your preferred doneness).

> **• VARIATIONS •**
>
> **COOKING POTATOES:** Place raw diced potatoes in a mug, cover with water, microwave for 3 to 5 minutes until tender. Drain and proceed as written.

Oklahoma Cheese Grits

MAKES 1 MUG

This recipe is based on the classic middle-American grits casserole. The egg makes it lighter and fluffier than the Southern version.

INGREDIENTS

¾ cup water

3 tablespoons quick-cooking grits

¼ teaspoon kosher salt

¼ teaspoon freshly ground black pepper, plus more for garnish

¼ cup grated sharp cheddar cheese

Dash of Worcestershire sauce

Dash of Tabasco sauce

1 large egg

Chopped scallion, for garnish

METHOD

1. Combine the water and grits in a jumbo mug. Cover loosely with plastic wrap and microwave for 2 minutes. Set aside for 10 minutes to allow the grits to absorb the water, cook again until all the liquid has been absorbed, another 1 to 2 minutes.

2. Stir in the salt, pepper, cheese, Worcestershire, Tabasco, and egg. Return to the microwave and cook for another 1 to 2 minutes until risen and firm. Serve immediately topped with chopped scallion and more black pepper.

• VARIATIONS •

CHEESE OPTIONS: Try this with goat cheese or Pepper Jack.

SPICE IT UP: Add 1–2 tablespoons of chopped fresh jalapeño or diced canned green chiles.

SHRIMP: Simulate this classic pair with the addition of ¼ cup of chopped cooked shrimp. If necessary, you can cook raw shrimp first: Cover in water and microwave for 2 to 3 minutes, then drain and chop.

Hangtown Fry

MAKES 1 MUG

The story of this dish takes place in Placerville, California, known as "Hangtown" during the Gold Rush. A high-rollin' miner told the chef of the local hotel to make him the most expensive thing he could think of. Eggs were precious because they were difficult to transport. Bacon was imported from the East, and oysters were brought in on ice from the coast.

INGREDIENTS

1 slice bacon, diced

½ scallion, minced

3 to 4 oysters, canned or fresh

1 tablespoon all-purpose flour

1 large egg

1 tablespoon whole milk

¼ teaspoon kosher salt

¼ teaspoon freshly ground black pepper

METHOD

1. Combine the bacon and scallion in a large mug. Microwave for 1 to 2 minutes, stirring intermittently, until the bacon is crispy and fat has rendered. Pour off all but 1 tablespoon of the bacon fat. Toss the oysters in the flour, shake off the excess, then stir them into the mug. Cook another minute, in the same manner, until the oysters begin to firm up.

2. In a separate mug, whisk together the egg, milk, salt, and pepper until frothy, then stir into the oyster mug. Microwave for another 1 to 2 minutes until the eggs are set. Serve immediately.

> • VARIATIONS •
>
> **MUSHROOMS:** Increase the umami effect by adding mushrooms (button, crimini, shitaki) and cooking them with the bacon.

Joe's Special

There are a number of San Francisco restaurants that claim to be the originator of this recipe. I salute whoever is responsible. This is one of the most satisfying morning bites, especially if you're watching your carb intake.

INGREDIENTS

1 teaspoon olive oil

1 tablespoon chopped onion

½ teaspoon dried oregano

½ cup ground beef

1 to 2 chopped mushrooms

½ cup chopped fresh baby spinach

1 large egg

Pinch of freshly grated nutmeg

¼ teaspoon kosher salt

¼ teaspoon freshly ground black pepper

METHOD

1. In a jumbo mug, combine the oil, onion, and oregano and microwave for 1 to 2 minutes until the onion has softened. Add the ground beef, mushrooms, and spinach and microwave again for 1 to 2 minutes, stirring in 30-second intervals, until the meat has cooked through. Pour off all but 1 tablespoon of the fat.

2. In a separate mug, whisk together the egg, nutmeg, salt, and pepper with a fork until frothy. Stir the egg mixture into the beef mug, and cook again for another 1 to 2 minutes until the egg is firm.

Cheese Soufflé

The soufflé is traditionally held up as the epitome of technical, touchy cooking. That's because they are delicate, and will eventually fall. The microwave version falls faster than the traditional oven-baked version, because it is cooked at a lower temperature. But this, as you will see, doesn't make it any less delicious. Don't let your preconceived notions prevent you from enjoying the deliciousness that is a cheese soufflé.

INGREDIENTS

1 tablespoon unsalted butter

1 tablespoon all-purpose flour

¼ teaspoon dry mustard

¼ teaspoon granulated garlic

¼ teaspoon kosher salt

¼ teaspoon freshly ground black pepper

¼ cup whole milk

½ cup grated sharp cheddar cheese

½ cup grated Swiss cheese

1 large egg, separated

METHOD

1. Put the butter in a large mug and microwave for 30 to 60 seconds until melted. Stir in the flour, mustard, garlic, salt and pepper. Heat another 30 seconds, then stir in the milk and heat again, for 30 seconds. Cool slightly, then stir in the cheese and the egg yolk quickly so that the egg doesn't cook in the heat of the butter.

2. In a separate small bowl, whip the egg white to stiff peaks using a whisk, or whip in a mug using a handheld milk foamer. Fold the egg white into the cheesy egg mixture and microwave for 1½ to 2½ minutes until the soufflé has risen high above the mug. Serve immediately.

VARIATIONS

HERBY: Brighten this recipe up with the addition of 2 tablespoons of chopped fresh herbs. Try flat-leaf parsley, chervil, thyme, tarragon, chives, or a combination.

MEATY: Add ¼ cup of chopped diced meat with the cheese. Try ham, bacon, prosciutto, or any leftover cooked meat you may have on hand.

CHOCOLATY: Yes, this can become a dessert. Replace the mustard, garlic, and pepper with 2 tablespoon of sugar and ¼ teaspoon of vanilla. Then replace the cheese with ¼ cup of melted chocolate chips.

Cheesy Two-Egg Mug Omelet

MAKES 1 MUG

An omelet is a very personal breakfast, and it is very easy to make it your own. This is my favorite, but there are innumerable options, as you will see in the variations below.

INGREDIENTS

1 tablespoon unsalted butter

1 tablespoon chopped scallion

¼ teaspoon dried herbes de Provence or dried thyme

1 tablespoon whole milk

2 large eggs

Pinch of kosher salt

Pinch of freshly ground black pepper

½ cup grated cheddar cheese

METHOD

1. In a large mug, combine the butter, scallion, and herbes de Provence and microwave for 1 minute until the butter has melted. Add the milk and eggs and whisk until frothy. Stir in the salt, pepper, and cheese. Microwave for another 1 to 2 minutes until the egg is firm. Serve immediately.

• VARIATIONS •

MUSHROOMS: Add ¼ cup of chopped cremini, shiitake, or white button mushrooms to the butter and scallion.

DENVER: Add ¼ cup of chopped ham, 2 tablespoons of chopped red or green bell pepper, and ¼ cup chopped yellow onion to the butter at the beginning of the recipe.

CHEESE OPTIONS: Any cheese you like can make a great omelet. Try something new by using goat, feta, or blue cheese. This is also a great place to use up that leftover cheese from the cheese plate you served at last night's party.

Huevos Rancheros

MAKES 1 MUG

A standard on many diner menus, huevos rancheros starts your morning off with a kick. The size of the kick is up to you. Choose a mild or spicy salsa to fit your morning mood.

INGREDIENTS

1 tablespoon olive oil

½ scallion, chopped

½ cup chopped tomatoes

¼ teaspoon ground cumin

½ avocado, diced

2 tablespoons salsa

1 tablespoon fresh cilantro, chopped

Dash of Tabasco sauce

¼ cup grated cheddar cheese

1 large egg

¼ teaspoon kosher salt

¼ teaspoon freshly ground black pepper

5 to 6 tortilla chips

Sour cream, for serving

METHOD

1. In a jumbo mug, combine the oil, scallion, tomato, cumin, and heat in the microwave for 1 minute until scallion is translucent and the tomato softened. Stir in the avocado, salsa, cilantro, Tabasco, cheese, egg, salt, and pepper. Insert the tortilla chips and nestle them down into the egg mixture. Microwave for another 1 to 2 minutes until the egg has set. Serve immediately with a dollop of sour cream.

• VARIATIONS •

MEAT: Add ¼ cup of chopped leftover carne asada, chicken, turkey, or shrimp for a heartier huevo.

CHEESE OPTIONS: Try this recipe with Monterey Jack, Pepper Jack, goat, feta, or authentic Mexican cotija cheese.

Spanish Tortilla

In Spain a tortilla is not a flat bread, but a loaded frittata, usually with potato. It is all the best stuff of breakfast rolled into one mug.

INGREDIENTS

1 tablespoon olive oil

¼ cup seeded and diced red bell pepper

¼ cup diced yellow onion

¼ teaspoon minced garlic

½ cup diced red or white potato

1 tablespoon whole milk

1 large egg

1 tablespoon minced fresh flat-leaf parsley

Pinch of kosher salt

Pinch of freshly ground black pepper

METHOD

1. In a jumbo mug, combine the oil, bell pepper, onion, garlic, and potato. Microwave for 3 to 5 minutes until the potato is tender. Stir in the milk, then add the egg, parsley, salt, and black pepper until well combined. Microwave for another 1 to 2 minutes until the egg is cooked through. Serve immediately.

• VARIATIONS •

SAFFRON: If you want to kick up the Spanish element in this recipe, add 2 to 3 threads of saffron to the oil. It will infuse the oil with its elegant essence and imbue it with a bright yellow color.

MEATY OPTIONS: Make this dish heartier (if that is even possible) with the addition of cooked Spanish chorizo, Italian sausage, or a salty cured meat like salami, pepperoni, or ham.

Strata

MAKES 1 MUG

This dish is named for the layers of ingredients that become visible when it is sliced out of a casserole dish. But for our mug purposes, it helps to think of it as basically a savory bread pudding.

INGREDIENTS

1 slice bacon, diced

1 tablespoon minced scallion

½ teaspoon dried Italian seasoning

1½ to 2 slices French bread, cubed (but you can use any bread)

½ cup grated fontina, cheddar, or Jack cheese

1 large egg

¼ cup whole milk

Pinch of freshly grated nutmeg

¼ teaspoon kosher salt

METHOD

1. Put the bacon, scallion, and Italian seasoning in a large mug and microwave for 1–2 minutes, stirring intermittently, until the bacon is cooked and the fat has rendered. Stir in the cubed bread and cheese and set aside.

2. In a separate mug, whisk together the egg, milk, nutmeg, and salt. Pour over the cubed bread and let sit for a minute or two, squishing the bread down so that it all gets saturated with the custard. Microwave for 1 to 3 minutes until risen and firm.

• VARIATIONS •

MEATY OPTIONS: You can easily replace the bacon with sausage, ham, or anything you happen to have on hand.

MEATLESS: Omit the meat altogether, and cook the scallion for a minute with a tablespoon of butter or olive oil.

CHEESY OPTIONS: Any cheese you like will work. Use what you have on hand.

Sausage Gravy and Biscuit

Yes, your dreams have come true! You can absolutely make a biscuit in the microwave. This stick-to-your-ribs breakfast specialty is only one of the uses for this fluffy technology. (See Old-fashioned Pot Pie on page 78, and Rhubarb Cobbler on page 168.)

INGREDIENTS

Biscuit

½ cup all-purpose flour

¼ teaspoon baking powder

⅛ teaspoon sugar

Pinch of kosher salt

3 tablespoons unsalted butter, chilled

2 tablespoons buttermilk (or regular milk)

Sausage Gravy

1 small link or patty of uncooked breakfast sausage, crumbled

1 tablespoon diced yellow onion

¼ teaspoon dried thyme or sage

1 tablespoon all-purpose flour

METHOD

1. *To make the biscuit:* In a jumbo mug, combine the flour, baking powder, sugar, and salt. Add the butter and cut it in with a fork until the mixture resembles coarse crumbs. Stir in the buttermilk and mix just until combined. Microwave for 1 to 2 minutes until risen and firm.

2. *To make the gravy:* In a second large mug, combine the sausage, onion, and thyme. Microwave for 1 to 2 minutes until the sausage has cooked through, and the fat has rendered. Pour off all but 1 tablespoon of the fat. Stir in the flour, salt, and pepper to create a paste. Slowly stir in enough milk to create a saucy consistency. Microwave for 2 to 3 minutes, stirring at 30-second intervals, until the gravy has thickened.

3. Break open the biscuit, pour in the gravy, and serve immediately.

(continued)

Sausage Gravy and Biscuit (continued)

Pinch of kosher salt

Pinch of freshly ground black pepper

½ to 1 cup whole milk

• VARIATIONS •

ADD AN EGG: Traditionally this is an egg-less breakfast, but adding an egg elevates this dish from homey to hearty. After the gravy is poured onto the biscuit, crack an egg into the empty gravy mug, whisk it up with a fork, and microwave for 1 to 2 minutes until it is cooked the way you like it.

SAUSAGE: Though ordinary breakfast sausage is the norm, any sausage will do. Try this with chorizo, Italian, or Polish sausages. You can even use precooked vegetarian sausages, but you will need to add ½ teaspoon of olive oil or butter to help the onion cook.

Warm Breakfast Spinach Salad

MAKES 1 MUG

Breakfast salads are sweeping the nation—or at least the trendy hipster cafes of California. But despite my initial eye rolling, the warm dressing and soft poached egg really do enhance the wilted greens in a delightful way. You need not have a handlebar mustache to enjoy it.

INGREDIENTS

1 tablespoon olive oil

1 tablespoon chopped red onion

1 teaspoon chopped fresh basil

¼ cup chopped prosciutto (or other cured meat you have on hand)

2 teaspoons balsamic vinegar

¼ teaspoon salt

¼ teaspoon freshly ground black pepper

Pinch of sugar

3 to 4 cherry tomatoes, halved

1 cup mixed baby greens, or spinach

1 teaspoon water

1 large egg

METHOD

1. In a jumbo mug, combine the oil, onion, basil, and prosciutto. Microwave for 1 to 2 minutes until the onion is tender. Stir in the balsamic vinegar, salt, pepper, and sugar until well blended. Add the tomatoes and mixed greens and toss until well coated.

2. To a second small mug, add a teaspoon of water, then crack in the egg, being careful not to break the yolk. Microwave for 30 to 60 seconds until the egg white is firm but the yolk is still runny (or cook to your preferred doneness). Slide the egg on top of the warm greens, and serve.

Shakshuka

Shakshuka, the name of this spicy, tomatoey egg dish, means "mixture" in Arabic slang. Its origin is claimed by many countries, including Israel and Tunisia. It likely has Berber origins, which means it traveled, and found a home in many places.

INGREDIENTS

1 tablespoon olive oil

1 tablespoon diced yellow onion

1 tablespoon seeded and chopped red or green bell pepper

2 tablespoons harissa (or 2 to 3 dashes of your favorite hot sauce)

½ garlic clove, minced

¼ teaspoon ground cumin

¼ teaspoon ground caraway

½ teaspoon Hungarian paprika

1 cup canned crushed tomatoes

¼ teaspoon kosher salt

¼ teaspoon freshly ground black pepper

¼ cup chopped spinach leaves

1 large egg

1 tablespoon crumbled feta cheese

METHOD

1. In a jumbo mug, combine the oil, onion, bell pepper, harissa, garlic, cumin, and caraway. Microwave for 1 to 2 minutes until the onion and bell pepper have softened. Stir in the paprika, crushed tomatoes, salt, black pepper, and spinach. Microwave for another 2 minutes to heat through.

2. Crack the egg carefully on top of the hot tomato sauce, trying not to break the yolk. Sprinkle a little water on top of the egg. Microwave for another 30 to 60 seconds, or until the egg white is firm but the yolk is still runny (or cook to your preferred doneness). Serve immediately, topped with crumbled feta cheese.

soups + stews

It's easy to open a can of soup or stew and microwave it. But if you have the ability to make it fresh, with no preservatives, less salt, and fresh ingredients, the results are 100 percent more satisfying.

Beef Barley Soup

MAKES 1 MUG

Barley is an underappreciated grain, and is rarely seen outside of a soup bowl. After you make this, try the barley recipe in Chapter 7 (page 133), and join my barley fan club.

INGREDIENTS

¼ cup barley

1 tablespoon olive oil

2 tablespoons chopped yellow onion

2 tablespoons chopped celery

1 tablespoon chopped carrot

2 to 3 white button mushrooms, chopped

¼ teaspoon dried thyme

½ cup shredded or diced cooked beef (use leftover roast or steak)

¼ teaspoon kosher salt

¼ teaspoon freshly ground black pepper

¼ cup minced fresh flat-leaf parsley

METHOD

1. In a large mug, combine the barley with enough water to cover. Cover loosely with plastic wrap and microwave for 3 to 5 minutes. Set aside to soak for 30 minutes, then cook again for 3 to 5 minutes until tender. Drain and reserve.

2. In a second large mug, combine the oil, onion, celery, carrot, mushrooms, and thyme. Microwave for 1 to 2 minutes until the vegetables are tender. Add the beef, salt, pepper, drained barley, and enough water to cover. Microwave for another 1 to 2 minutes until heated through. Stir in the parsley and serve immediately.

• VARIATIONS •

RAW BEEF: If you have no leftover cooked meat, you can easily cook some in a microwave before you start the recipe. Combine ½ teaspoon of olive oil with ½ cup of diced beef (sirloin, chuck roast, or stew meat) and microwave for 2 to 3 minutes until cooked through. Then continue with the recipe as directed.

Albóndigas

These meatballs are Arabic in origin, by way of Spain, and then translated to Hispanic America. Meatball making in a mug is by no means impossible, but this first recipe avoids the task by simply using ready-made sausage. For the scratch technique, see the Scratch Mug Meatball recipe page 48.

INGREDIENTS

1 small red or white potato, diced

1 Italian sausage, sliced into ½-inch chunks (leave the casing on)

2 tablespoons chopped yellow onion

1 serrano or jalapeño chile, seeded and minced

¼ teaspoon ground cumin

¼ teaspoon dried oregano

2 tablespoons chopped celery

1 tablespoon chopped carrot

¼ cup grated or diced zucchini

¼ teaspoon kosher salt

¼ teaspoon freshly ground black pepper

½ cup diced tomatoes

¼ cup minced fresh cilantro leaves

METHOD

1. In a large mug, stir together the potatoes with enough water to cover. Cover loosely with plastic wrap and microwave for 3 to 5 minutes, until tender. Drain and set aside.

2. In a jumbo mug, combine the sausage, onion, chile, cumin, oregano, celery, and carrot. Microwave for 5 to 8 minutes until the sausage has cooked through, the fat has rendered, and the vegetables have softened. Add the drained potatoes, zucchini, salt, black pepper, tomatoes, and enough water to fill the mug and stir to combine. Microwave another 30 to 60 seconds until heated through. Top with the minced cilantro and serve immediately.

SCRATCH MUG MEATBALLS

MAKES 12–15 MEATBALLS

These are a great alternative to greasy Italian sausage. Make these meatballs, freeze them, then pop them into your mug the next time you want this South-of-the-Border classic.

INGREDIENTS

½ cup bread crumbs (save your bread heels for a cheap and easy source of bread crumbs)

½ cup chopped scallion

½ pound ground meat (¼ pound each pork and beef is best)

¼ cup cooked rice

½ teaspoon ground cumin

¼ cup chopped fresh cilantro

¼ teaspoon kosher salt

½ teaspoon dried oregano

1 egg white

METHOD

1. Combine all the ingredients in a large bowl. Mix thoroughly, then form into small meatballs. Place the balls on a baking sheet and freeze solid. When frozen, transfer to a ziplock bag (so that they will maintain their shape). Store in freezer for up to several months.

2. To use, microwave 3 to 4 balls in a large mug with a 2 to 3 tablespoons of water for 3 to 5 minutes until cooked through. Follow the Albóndigas recipe, simply use the meatballs in place of the Italian sausage, and cook as directed.

Chicken Soup with Rice

MAKES 1 MUG

Forget the NyQuil or Alka-Seltzer. If you feel a cold coming on, grab a mug and self-medicate with this easy remedy.

INGREDIENTS

¼ cup white or brown rice

1 tablespoon olive oil

2 tablespoons chopped yellow onion

2 tablespoons chopped celery

1 tablespoon chopped carrot

¼ teaspoon dried thyme

½ cup cooked chicken (use leftover or canned chicken), shredded or diced

¼ teaspoon kosher salt

¼ teaspoon freshly ground black pepper

2 tablespoons minced fresh flat-leaf parsley

METHOD

1. In a jumbo mug, combine the rice with enough water to cover. Cover loosely with plastic wrap and microwave for 5 to 8 minutes until tender. Set aside.

2. In a large mug, combine the oil, onion, celery, carrot, and thyme. Microwave for 1 to 2 minutes until the vegetables are tender. Add the chicken, salt, pepper, parsley, cooked rice, and more water, if needed, to fill the mug. Microwave for another 1 to 2 minutes until heated through.

• VARIATIONS •

LEFTOVER RICE: If you have cooked rice on hand, omit the first step in this recipe, and simply add the cooked rice to the mug along with the cooked chicken.

RAW CHICKEN: If you have no cooked chicken on hand, you can cook diced raw meat in the microwave. Combine ½ cup of diced breast meat with 1 tablespoon of oil in a large mug and microwave for 2 to 3 minutes until cooked through. Then add it to the recipe as directed.

Chicken and Dumpling

This old-home recipe is quintessential comfort food. This dumpling is really just a loose biscuit, and is easily enjoyed on its own, minus the chicken. See the Variations below for the how-to.

INGREDIENTS

Chicken

1 tablespoon olive oil

2 tablespoons chopped yellow onion

2 tablespoons chopped celery

1 tablespoon chopped carrot

¼ teaspoon dried thyme

½ cup cooked chicken (use leftover or canned chicken), shredded or diced

¼ teaspoon kosher salt

¼ teaspoon freshly ground black pepper

2 tablespoons minced fresh flat-leaf parsley

(continued)

METHOD

1. *To make the chicken:* In a large mug, combine the oil, onion, celery, carrot, and thyme. Microwave for 1 to 2 minutes until the vegetables are tender. Add the chicken, salt, pepper, parsley, and enough water to cover. Microwave for another 1 to 2 minutes until heated through.

2. *To make the dumpling:* In a second mug, combine the flour, baking powder, and salt. Add the butter and cut it in with a fork until the mixture resembles coarse crumbs. Add in the milk and stir just until combined. Dollop the dough into the chicken soup mug, and microwave for 30 to 60 seconds until risen and firm.

Dumpling

2 tablespoons all-purpose flour

⅛ teaspoon baking powder

Pinch of kosher salt

1½ teaspoons unsalted butter, chilled

1 tablespoon whole milk

• VARIATIONS •

CHEESY: Add ¼ cup grated cheese (cheddar, Jack, or whatever cheese you have on hand) to the dumpling mixture along with the flour, and before the butter is cut in. Then proceed with the recipe as directed.

HERBY: Add ¼ cup of chopped fresh herbs to the flour before the butter is cut in. Then proceed with the recipe as directed

CHICKEN-FREE: Make the dumpling as directed, and cook in a simple, ready-made vegetarian broth.

Egg Drop Soup

Also known as "egg flower soup," the wispy garnish is made by stirring in a drizzle of eggs to the hot broth. It is frequently thickened with the addition of cornstarch, but in a mug, I find the starchiness overpowering.

INGREDIENTS

1 cup chicken broth plus 1 tablespoon

¼ teaspoon finely grated fresh ginger

1 teaspoon soy sauce

1 tablespoon chopped scallions

¼ teaspoon kosher salt

Pinch of white pepper

1 large egg, lightly beaten

METHOD

1. In a large mug, combine the 1 cup of broth with the ginger and soy sauce. Microwave for 1 minute to warm through. Add the scallions, salt, and pepper and microwave for another minute until very hot. Slowly drizzle the beaten egg into the hot broth while stirring. Microwave for another 30 to 60 seconds, if necessary, until the egg has set and warmed through. Serve immediately.

• VARIATIONS •

PROTEIN: The addition of ¼ cup of diced tofu or chicken turns this traditional appetizer soup into a main meal.

Chile Verde

MAKES 1 MUG

This bright, fresh, green version is a nice change of pace from the standard tomato-based chili. It typically uses lighter meats, but check out the variations below for a vegetarian version.

INGREDIENTS

1 tablespoon olive oil

2 tablespoons minced yellow onion

1 garlic clove, minced

2 tablespoons minced celery

1 tablespoon seeded and minced poblano, Anaheim, or jalapeño chile

¼ teaspoon ground cumin

⅛ teaspoon ground coriander

½ cup cooked pork or chicken meat, minced

1 tomatillo or small green tomato, diced

1 tablespoon minced fresh oregano leaves, or 1 teaspoon dried

¼ cup minced cilantro leaves

¼ teaspoon salt

¼ teaspoon freshly ground black pepper

Sour cream, for serving

METHOD

1. In a large mug, combine the oil, onion, garlic, celery, chile, cumin, and coriander. Microwave for 1 to 2 minutes until the vegetables are tender.

2. Add the meat, tomatillo, oregano, cilantro, salt, pepper, and enough water to cover. Microwave for another 1 to 2 minutes until heated through. Serve immediately with a dollop of sour cream.

• VARIATIONS •

BEANS: If you like your chili with beans, add ¼ cup of rinsed and drained canned white beans to the mix when the meat is added.

VEGETARIAN VERDE: Omit the meat altogether and add, instead, ½ cup of rinsed and drained canned white or garbanzo beans in its place.

RAW MEAT: Combine ½ cup of raw diced pork (shoulder, butt, or loin) or chicken breast with 1 teaspoon of oil in a large mug. Microwave for 2 to 3 minutes until cooked through. Then add it to the recipe as directed.

Chili Con Carne

MAKES 1 MUG

Nothing warms you up on a cold afternoon like a mug of hot chili. That said, it's pretty darn good in the summer, too.

INGREDIENTS

1 tablespoon olive oil

½ cup ground beef

2 tablespoons minced yellow onion

1 garlic clove, minced

2 tablespoons minced celery

1 tablespoon minced canned chipotle chile

¼ teaspoon ground cumin

⅛ teaspoon ground coriander

1 teaspoon tomato paste

¼ cup diced tomato

¼ cup canned kidney beans

1 tablespoon minced fresh oregano leaves, or 1 teaspoon dried

¼ teaspoon kosher salt

¼ teaspoon freshly ground black pepper

1 tablespoon grated cheddar cheese

1 tablespoon sour cream

METHOD

1. In a jumbo mug, combine the oil, beef, onion, garlic, celery, chile, cumin, and coriander. Microwave for 1 to 2 minutes until the vegetables are tender. Add the tomato paste and tomato and microwave for another minute to warm through.

2. Add the beans, oregano, salt, black pepper, and enough water to cover. Microwave for another 1 to 2 minutes until heated through. Serve immediately topped with the grated cheese and sour cream.

> **• VARIATIONS •**
>
> **MORE CHILE IN YOUR CHILI:** Instead of the chipotle and tomato paste, use canned enchilada sauce, or your own chile paste made from dried chiles that have been toasted, seeded, soaked, and pulverized.

Split Peas and Ham

Split peas are the dried edible seeds inside a pea pod, also known as legumes. But legumes take a long time to cook, and in the world of mug cookery, time is not something we are willing to take. So this shortcut, while not authentic, is sure to please your peas craving.

INGREDIENTS

1 tablespoon unsalted butter

¼ cup diced ham

¼ cup diced yellow onion

½ garlic clove, minced

1½ cups canned peas, drained

½ to 1 cup vegetable or chicken broth

¼ teaspoon kosher salt

¼ teaspoon freshly ground black pepper

Croutons or crackers, for serving

METHOD

1. In a large mug, combine the butter, ham, onion, and garlic. Microwave for 1 to 2 minutes until the butter has melted and the vegetables are tender.

2. Add the peas and smash them with a fork into a paste. Stir in broth until you reach a soupy consistency. Add the salt and pepper, and cook for another 1 to 2 minutes to warm through. Serve immediately with croutons or crackers.

Southwestern Corn Chowder

MAKES 1 MUG

Chowder has come to mean any chunky soup that is just a tad too thin to be called a stew. The name may come from the French *chaudière*, which is a type of stove that the first chowders were made on. Then again, some think it comes from *chauderée*, which is a fish stew from coastal regions of France. Regardless, I love sweet corn flavor paired with spicy chiles and herbs.

INGREDIENTS

1 small red or white potato

1 tablespoon unsalted butter

¼ cup chopped yellow onion

½ garlic clove, minced

¼ cup chopped celery

¼ teaspoon ground cumin

¼ teaspoon dried thyme

1 tablespoon all-purpose flour

½ cup whole milk

1 cup corn kernels (fresh, frozen, or drained canned)

1 to 2 tablespoons canned diced green chiles, or diced fresh jalapeño

¼ teaspoon kosher salt

¼ teaspoon freshly ground black pepper

1 tablespoon chopped fresh cilantro

METHOD

1. In a jumbo mug, combine the potato with enough water to cover. Loosely cover with plastic wrap and microwave for 3 to 5 minutes until tender. Drain and set aside.

2. In a large mug, combine the butter with the onion, garlic, celery, cumin, and thyme. Cook for 1 to 2 minutes until the butter has melted and the vegetables are tender. Stir in the flour to make a paste. Slowly stir in the milk. Add the drained potatoes, corn, chiles, salt, and black pepper and cook for another 1 to 2 minutes until heated through. Stir in the cilantro and serve immediately.

French Onion Soup

The key to great onion soup is twofold—delicious broth and well-caramelized onions. Because deep caramelization is hard to get in a microwave, a well-made broth here is crucial. If you are out of sherry, dry white wine, or a splash of white wine vinegar are acceptable substitutes.

INGREDIENTS

1 tablespoon unsalted butter

1 small yellow onion, diced (about 1 cup)

¼ teaspoon kosher salt

1 cup beef broth

1 tablespoon dry sherry

¼ teaspoon freshly ground black pepper

1 thick slice French bread (cut to fit into the top of the mug)

1 ounce grated Gruyère or Swiss cheese, about ¼ cup

METHOD

1. In a large mug, combine the butter, onion, and salt. Microwave for 1 to 2 minutes until the onions are tender and the butter begins to brown. Add the beef broth, sherry, pepper, and microwave for another 30 to 60 seconds to warm through.

2. Place the French bread on the top of the mug and press it into the liquid. Top with cheese and microwave for another 30 to 60 seconds to melt the cheese. Serve immediately.

• VARIATIONS •

VEGETARIAN: This is easily converted into a meat-free dish by substituting veggie broth. You can create the umami effect of the beef with the addition of 2 to 3 chopped shiitake mushrooms, either fresh or dried.

Minestrone

This is a classic example of peasant food, using whatever is on hand for a hearty, nutritious meal. If you have to run to the store for ingredients, you're not doing it right.

INGREDIENTS

¼ cup elbow macaroni, or another pasta or grain

1½ cups water

1 tablespoon olive oil

1 tablespoon chopped scallion

1 tablespoon chopped celery

1 tablespoon chopped carrot

1 teaspoon fresh oregano, or ¼ teaspoon of dried

1 teaspoon chopped fresh basil leaves

½ cup canned beans of your choice, rinsed and drained

¼ cup fresh or canned diced tomato

¼ teaspoon kosher salt

¼ teaspoon freshly ground black pepper

1 to 1½ cups vegetable or chicken broth, or water

1 tablespoon grated Parmesan cheese

METHOD

1. In a jumbo mug, combine the macaroni and water. Cover lightly with plastic wrap and microwave for 2 to 3 minutes. Set aside to absorb for 20 minutes, then microwave again, for 2 to 3 minutes until tender. Drain and set aside.

2. In a large mug, combine the oil with scallion, celery, carrot, oregano, and basil. Microwave for 1 to 2 minutes until vegetables are tender. Add the drained cooked pasta, beans, tomato, salt, pepper, and broth. Microwave for another 1 to 2 minutes until heated through. Serve immediately topped with the grated cheese.

Irish Stew

Just your basic stew, Irished-up with the use of lamb. Traditionally mutton was used, because economically only the old sheep, no longer viable as wool producers, were destined for the pot. Considering that you probably aren't raising wool, go ahead and use lamb or beef.

INGREDIENTS

1 small red or white potato

1 tablespoon olive oil

½ cup lamb or beef, diced (such as shank, leg meat, stew meat)

2 tablespoons minced leek or scallions

2 tablespoons minced carrot

¼ cup shredded green cabbage

¼ teaspoon kosher salt

¼ teaspoon freshly ground black pepper

1 to 2 cups beef stock

METHOD

1. In a jumbo mug, combine the potato with enough water to cover. Loosely cover with plastic wrap and microwave for 3 to 5 minutes until tender. Drain and set aside.

2. In a second large mug, combine oil with the lamb and leek and cook for 1 to 2 minutes until the meat is cooked through. Add the carrot, and cabbage and cook for another 1 to 2 minutes to soften the vegetables. Add the drained potatoes, salt, pepper, and beef stock to cover. Microwave for another minute until heated through. Serve immediately.

• VARIATIONS •

GUINNESS STEW: Replace half the stock with dark Guinness Stout for a super-Irish twist on this old favorite.

LEFTOVER LAMB OR BEEF: Instead of first cooking the meat with oil, simply add cooked meat at the end, along with the stock.

New England Clam Chowder

MAKES 1 MUG

I don't usually like ordering this dish from restaurants. It's almost always too thick. But when I make it myself I can give it just the right amount of viscosity. I'm looking for the texture of soup, not wallpaper paste.

INGREDIENTS

1 small red or white potato

1 tablespoon unsalted butter

¼ cup diced yellow onion

¼ cup diced celery

¼ teaspoon Old Bay seasoning

¼ teaspoon dried thyme

1 tablespoon all-purpose flour

1 cup whole milk

¼ cup clam juice or chicken stock

¼ cup canned chopped clams with juice (about ½ small can)

¼ teaspoon kosher salt

¼ teaspoon freshly ground black pepper

1 tablespoon chopped fresh flat-leaf parsley

METHOD

1. In a jumbo mug, combine the potato with enough water to cover. Loosely cover with plastic wrap and microwave for 3 to 5 minutes until tender. Drain and set aside.

2. In a large mug, combine the butter with the onion, celery, Old Bay, and thyme. Cook for 1 to 2 minutes until the butter has melted and the vegetables are tender. Stir in the flour to make a paste. Slowly stir in the milk and clam juice. Add the drained potatoes, clams, salt, and pepper and cook for another 1 to 2 minutes until heated through. Stir in the parsley and serve immediately.

• VARIATIONS •

MANHATTAN CLAM CHOWDER: Omit the flour and add ½ garlic clove to the butter. Replace the Old Bay with dried Italian seasoning, and replace the milk with an equal amount of canned or fresh chopped tomatoes.

Potato-Leek Soup

When it's cold, this dish is known as Vichyssoise. When it's hot, it's known as amazing.

INGREDIENTS

1 tablespoon unsalted butter

½ cup chopped leeks (or scallions)

¼ cup chopped celery

½ teaspoon dried herbes de Provence or dried thyme

1 tablespoon all-purpose flour

1 cup whole milk

1 cup mashed potatoes (see Mug Mash variation below)

¼ teaspoon kosher salt

¼ teaspoon freshly ground black pepper

METHOD

1. In a large mug, combine the butter with the leeks, celery, and herbs. Cook for 1 to 2 minutes until the butter has melted and the vegetables are tender. Stir in the flour to make a paste. Slowly stir in the milk. Add the potatoes, salt, and pepper, and cook for another 1 to 2 minutes until heated through. Stir in the parsley and serve immediately.

• VARIATIONS •

BACON: This recipe is often made with bacon instead of butter. Dice 1 slice of bacon, and cook it with the onion, celery, and herbs. Drain off all but 1 tablespoon of the fat before adding the flour.

MUG MASH: Make your own mash in the microwave. Cover a diced potato with water and heat for 3 to 5 minutes until soft. Mash it up with a fork before adding it to this recipe.

INSTANT POTATO: Don't be ashamed to use processed potato buds. They make this dish even quicker and easier. Make them according to the package instructions before adding them to the mug.

Vegetarian Black Bean Chili

MAKES 1 MUG

Black beans are the vegetarian's best friend. Thick and meaty in texture, but not overly beany, they give this dish just the right amount of backbone. Now, even vegetarians can satisfy their inner cowboy.

INGREDIENTS

1 tablespoon olive oil

¼ cup chopped yellow onion

½ garlic clove, minced

¼ cup chopped celery

¼ teaspoon ground cumin

2 tablespoons canned diced green chiles (or your favorite salsa)

¼ cup chopped fresh cilantro

½ cup chopped tomato

1 cup canned drained black beans

½ cup precooked white or brown rice

¼ teaspoon kosher salt

¼ teaspoon freshly ground black pepper

Sour cream, for serving

METHOD

1. In a large mug, combine the oil, onion, garlic, celery, and cumin. Microwave for 1 to 2 minutes until the vegetables are tender.

2. Add the chiles, cilantro, tomato, beans, rice, salt, and black pepper. Microwave for another 1 to 2 minutes to warm through. Serve immediately with a dollop of sour cream.

4

meaty traditions

The microwave was originally marketed as a full-on oven, with books full of recipes for large roasts of beef and turkey, meat loaf, and casseroles. But quickly the ovens' use shifted to tea water, popcorn, and the occasional baked potato. I think it's time to rediscover their use for cooking real food. Who's with me?

Beef Stroganoff

This old Russian recipe, which first appeared in print in the 1800s, has become an international standard. The sauce, traditionally thickened with flour, is lightened up here. This recipe calls for sirloin, but feel free to use any cut of beef you can lay your hands on. I'm pretty sure I enjoyed this made with ground beef once.

INGREDIENTS

¼ cup egg noodles

1 to 1½ cups water

1 tablespoon olive oil

¼ cup diced yellow onion

½ cup thinly sliced beef sirloin steak (2 to 3 ounces)

2 to 3 cremini or white button mushrooms, sliced

½ garlic clove, minced

⅛ teaspoon Worcestershire sauce

¼ teaspoon kosher salt

¼ teaspoon freshly ground black pepper

Sour cream, for serving

METHOD

1. In a large mug, combine the noodles with enough water to cover. Cover loosely with plastic wrap and microwave for 2 to 3 minutes. Set aside for 15 minutes to allow the noodles to absorb the water, then microwave again for 2 to 3 minutes until tender.

2. In a jumbo mug, combine the oil, onion, steak, and microwave for 2 to 3 minutes until the onions are tender and the meat has begun to cook through. Add the mushrooms, garlic, Worcestershire, salt, and pepper and microwave for another 1 to 2 minutes to heat through.

3. Drain the noodles and stir them into the mug of beef, along with the sour cream. Microwave for another 30 seconds, and serve.

All-American Meat Loaf

Everyone has a favorite version of meat loaf. Mine is ketchup-free, with just a hint of onion. If you're a ketchup head, feel free to augment this recipe, or choose one of the variations below.

INGREDIENTS

1 slice bread, torn into bits, or ½ cup cracker crumbs

2 tablespoons whole milk

½ teaspoon Worcestershire sauce

½ teaspoon granulated garlic

1 chopped scallion

¼ pound ground beef

¼ teaspoon kosher salt

¼ teaspoon freshly ground black pepper

METHOD

1. Combine the bread, milk, Worcestershire, and garlic in a large mug. Mix together well and let sit for 1 to 2 minutes until the bread has absorbed the liquid and softened.

2. Add the scallion, ground beef, salt, and pepper and mix thoroughly. Press the mixture so that it is level in the mug. Microwave for 4 to 5 minutes until the center is no longer pink. Let stand for a minute or two before serving.

> ### • VARIATIONS •
>
> **VEGETABLES:** You can add up to ½ cup of cooked, chopped vegetables, like carrots, mushrooms, or peppers.
>
> **ONION SOUP MIX:** My super secret shortcut is the addition of dry onion soup mix (which I think they now call "onion recipe mix"). For 1 mug meat loaf, omit the scallion, salt, and pepper, add 1 tablespoon of the soup mix, and combine well.
>
> **EGG:** For a softer, lighter meat loaf, add an egg. Whisk it up with a fork and add it to the milk in the beginning of the recipe.

Sausage and Peppers

MAKES 1 MUG

The key to this recipe is a good Italian sausage with lots of fennel. If your sausage is short on flavor, add an extra pinch of fennel seed.

INGREDIENTS

1 tablespoon olive oil

¼ cup sliced yellow onion

1 cup seeded and sliced bell peppers (use a variety of colored peppers if possible)

½ teaspoon dried Italian seasoning

¼ teaspoon kosher salt

¼ teaspoon freshly ground black pepper

1 Italian sausage, meat removed from casing and broken into 1-inch pieces

1 teaspoon red wine vinegar

1 tablespoon chopped fresh flat-leaf parsley

Crusty Italian bread, for serving

METHOD

1. In a large mug, combine the oil, onion, bell peppers, salt, and black pepper and microwave for 1 to 2 minutes until the vegetables are tender. Add the sausage and vinegar and microwave for another 3 to 5 minutes, stirring occasionally, until the meat is cooked through. Stir in the parsley, and serve immediately with a piece of crusty Italian bread.

Corned Beef and Cabbage

A Saint Patty's Day specialty, it is rare to see this dish outside the month of March. I'm on a mission to change that trend, one mug at a time.

INGREDIENTS

1 small red or white potato, diced

1 tablespoon olive oil

¼ cup diced yellow onion

½ cup shredded green cabbage

¼ teaspoon kosher salt

¼ teaspoon freshly ground black pepper

1 cup shredded or diced prepared corned beef

Spicy mustard, for serving

METHOD

1. In a large mug, combine the potatoes with enough water to cover. Cover loosely with plastic wrap and microwave for 3 to 5 minutes until tender. Drain and set aside.

2. In a second large mug, combine the oil, onion, cabbage, salt, and pepper and microwave for 2 to 3 minutes until the vegetables are tender. Add the corned beef and potato, and microwave for another 30 to 60 seconds to warm through. Serve immediately with a side of spicy mustard.

Cheesy Burger

MAKES 1 MUG

While this is not a really a burger, it has all the elements. And, if you use a mug with a wide enough bottom, it can easily be popped out onto a bun. So actually, it really is a burger!

INGREDIENTS

¼ *pound ground beef*

¼ *cup chopped yellow onion*

¼ *teaspoon kosher salt*

¼ *teaspoon freshly ground black pepper*

¼ *cup cheddar cheese (Or your favorite cheese. Try blue, goat, feta, and brie!)*

¼ *cup chopped tomato*

¼ *cup shredded lettuce*

1 *tablespoon chopped red onion*

1 *chopped pickle*

Ketchup, mustard, and mayo as needed

METHOD

1. In a large mug, stir together the beef, yellow onion, salt, and pepper. Press it flat, and poke a finger-sized hole in the center to keep it from rising during cooking. Microwave for 2 to 3 minutes until the beef is cooked through. Pour off the excess fat. Place the cheese on top and cook again until melted, 30 to 60 seconds more. Serve immediately topped with tomato, lettuce, red onion, pickle, and condiments as desired.

• VARIATIONS •

ON A BUN: Instead of eating this patty out of a mug, cook it in a wide-bottomed mug and invert it onto a bun and layer with the tomato, lettuce, onion, pickle, and condiments.

MUSHROOM BURGER: Put 2 to 3 sliced cremini or white button mushrooms in the mug with 1 teaspoon of oil and microwave for 1 to 2 minutes until tender. Stir in the remaining ingredients and continue with the recipe as written.

JALAPEÑO BURGER: Put 1 sliced jalapeño chile in the mug with 1 teaspoon of oil and microwave for 1 to 2 minutes until tender. Stir in the remaining ingredients and continue with the recipe as written.

Corn Dog

Unless you have a very tall and skinny mug, this recipe will not look like the traditional corn dog you're used to. It will, however, taste like it, which is all that really matters.

INGREDIENTS

1 tablespoon unsalted butter

½ cup whole milk

1 large egg

½ cup cornmeal

½ cup all-purpose flour

1 teaspoon baking powder

¼ teaspoon sugar

¼ teaspoon kosher salt

¼ teaspoon freshly ground black pepper

1 hot dog, cut into ½-inch slices

Mustard, for serving

METHOD

1. Put the butter in a large mug and microwave for 30 to 60 seconds until melted. Stir in the milk and egg, and beat with a fork until well combined. Add the cornmeal, flour, baking powder, sugar, salt, pepper and mix to form a batter. Fold in the hot dog slices. Microwave until the batter is risen and firm, 1½ to 2½ minutes. Serve immediately with mustard.

• VARIATIONS •

CHEESY DOG: Add ¼ cup grated cheddar cheese along with the hot dog slices, and cook as directed.

POLISH DOG: Replace the hot dog with your favorite sausage. Try kielbasa, andouille, Italian, or even veggie sausages. Be sure they are fully cooked before you fold them into the corn bread batter.

Old-Fashioned Pot Pie

MAKES 1 MUG

Making pot pie in a microwave is as easy as . . . well, it's really easy. You can use store-bought puff or make your own pie dough. The recipe for the homemade dough (see page 80) can be made ahead of time, kept in the freezer, and pulled out as necessary for those midnight pot pie cravings—which are not at all weird.

INGREDIENTS

1 tablespoon unsalted butter

2 tablespoons diced onion

2 tablespoons diced celery

2 tablespoons diced carrot

2 tablespoons fresh or frozen peas

¼ teaspoon dried thyme

1 teaspoon all-purpose flour

½ cup whole milk

1 cup cooked chicken (use leftover or canned chicken), shredded or diced

¼ teaspoon kosher salt

¼ teaspoon freshly ground black pepper

2 tablespoons minced fresh flat-leaf parsley

One 3-inch piece frozen puff pastry, or pie dough, still frozen

METHOD

1. In a large mug, combine the butter, onion, celery, carrot, peas, and thyme. Microwave for 1 to 2 minutes until the vegetables are tender. Stir in the flour to make a paste, then slowly stir in the milk.

2. Add the chicken, salt, pepper, and parsley and toss to coat. Top the mug with the dough and microwave again until the dough is cooked and firm, 30 to 60 seconds. Serve immediately.

• VARIATIONS •

BISCUIT-TOPPED POT PIE: Replace the pastry with the biscuit from Sausage Gravy and Biscuit recipe on page 38.

ANOTHER MEAT: Any meat can become a pie. In fact, throughout history there is a very long tradition of meat pie making. Just be sure the meat you add to your mug is precooked.

PIE DOUGH

Any pie dough will cook in the microwave, but I prefer to make mine whole wheat. The brown color makes up for the lack of browning that zapping cannot create.

INGREDIENTS

¼ to ½ cup ice water

1 teaspoon fresh lemon juice or apple cider vinegar

1½ cups whole wheat, all-purpose, or gluten-free flour

Pinch of kosher salt

1 tablespoon granulated sugar

8 tablespoons (1 stick) unsalted butter, diced and chilled

METHOD

1. Combine the water and lemon juice in a cup and set aside. In a medium bowl, stir together the flour, salt, and sugar with a fork. Add the chilled butter and break it into pieces using a fork or your fingertips until the mixture resembles a coarse meal; the mixture should not be creamy. Stir in 2 to 3 tablespoons of ice water to moisten flour. Add enough additional water just to hold the dough together; the dough should look marbled, with bits of flour and butter still visible. Press the dough into a disk, wrap it in plastic, and refrigerate for at least an hour. Overnight is better. (The dough will keep in the fridge for 2 days, or can be frozen for several weeks.)

2. To roll out the dough, divide it into 2 to 3 smaller pieces. Work with one piece at a time, and keep the rest refrigerated. Knead the dough briefly into a flattened disk, and place on a well-floured surface. Roll with a rolling pin over the center of the dough, moving in one direction only. Turn the dough 90 degrees, and roll in the center again. Turn the dough again and repeat this pattern until the dough is

¼ inch thick. Turning the dough in this manner alerts you right away if it starts sticking to the counter. Spread flour under the dough as necessary to prevent sticking. Work quickly to keep the dough from warming up. Using a cookie or biscuit cutter, cut the dough into 3-inch circles (to fit the top of your mug). Using a fork, poke tiny decorative holes in the dough. This will keep the dough from bubbling up as it cooks. Place the circles in a single layer on a wax paper–lined baking sheet, seal in plastic wrap, and freeze solid. As needed, cook as directed, using one disk of dough for the top of each mug pie.

Pork Chop and Applesauce

Meat and fruit have a long history of togetherness. Apples, especially, offset the richness of pork, with their crisp, tart flavor. If you grew up in the 1970s, this dish will forever be associated with TV's *The Brady Bunch*.

INGREDIENTS

1 small Fuji apple, peeled, cored, and diced

¼ teaspoon ground cinnamon

1 tablespoon unsalted butter

¼ cup diced yellow onion

1 garlic clove, minced

1 teaspoon fresh or dried sage

¼ teaspoon kosher salt

¼ teaspoon freshly ground black pepper

One 2- to 3-ounce boneless pork cutlet, diced

Sour cream, for serving

METHOD

1. In a large mug, combine the apples and cinnamon with enough water to cover. Cover loosely with plastic wrap and microwave for 5 to 8 minutes until tender. Drain and set aside.

2. In a second large mug, combine the butter, onion, garlic, sage, salt, pepper, and pork and microwave for 2 to 3 minutes until the vegetables are tender and the meat is cooked through. Add the drained apples and microwave for another 30 to 60 seconds to warm through. Serve immediately with a dollop of sour cream.

Shepherd's Pie

True shepherd's pie is made with mutton (which is a really old sheep). But because in the U.S. we are cowboys and not sheep farmers, it is usually made here with beef. If you find it in Britain made with beef, it will usually be called "cottage pie."

INGREDIENTS

1½ tablespoons unsalted butter

2 tablespoons diced yellow onion

2 tablespoons diced celery

2 tablespoons diced carrot

2 tablespoons fresh or frozen peas

¼ teaspoon dried sage

1 cup ground lamb or beef

¼ teaspoon kosher salt

¼ teaspoon freshly ground black pepper

2 tablespoons minced fresh flat-leaf parsley

½ cup mashed potatoes (see Mug Mash page 65)

1 tablespoon grated Parmesan cheese

METHOD

1. In a jumbo mug, combine 1 tablespoon of the butter, the onion, celery, carrot, and peas, and sage. Microwave for 1 to 2 minutes until the vegetables are tender. Stir in the lamb, salt, pepper, and parsley and cook again until the meat is cooked through, 3 to 4 minutes. Top the mug with the mashed potatoes, the remaining ½ tablespoon butter, and the grated cheese. Microwave again for 30 to 60 seconds to warm the potatoes. Serve immediately.

Swedish Meatballs

Meatballs were brought to Scandinavia by Charles XII of Sweden, after his exile in Istanbul. The Swedes usually include allspice in their meatballs, and serve them in a thick sauce with a side of lingonberry jam and pickles. If you can't find lingonberry jam in your supermarket, try Ikea.

INGREDIENTS

Meatball

1 slice bread, torn into bits

2 tablespoons whole milk

¼ cup chopped yellow onion

¼ pound ground beef

¼ teaspoon each: salt, freshly ground pepper, ground allspice, ground ginger, and freshly grated nutmeg

Sauce

1 tablespoon unsalted butter

1 tablespoon all-purpose flour

¼ cup beef broth

¼ cup sour cream

¼ teaspoon kosher salt

¼ teaspoon freshly ground black pepper

1 tablespoon minced fresh flat-leaf parsley

METHOD

1. *To make the meatball:* Combine the bread and milk in a large mug. Mix together well and let sit for 1 to 2 minutes until the bread has absorbed the liquid and softened.

2. Add the onion, ground beef, salt, pepper, allspice, ginger, and nutmeg and mix thoroughly. Microwave for 4 to 5 minutes until the center of the meat mixture is no longer pink. Set aside.

3. *To make the sauce:* Put the butter in a separate mug and microwave for 30 to 60 seconds until melted. Stir in the flour to make a paste, then slowly stir in the broth, sour cream, salt, pepper, and parsley. Microwave for 1 to 2 minutes to warm and thicken, then pour over the meatball and serve.

Tamale Pie

Neither a tamale nor a pie, this American interpretation, as inauthentic as it is, happens to be really good. Say what you will, we are a creative people.

INGREDIENTS

Filling

1 tablespoon unsalted butter

2 tablespoons diced yellow onion

1 small tomato, diced

1 teaspoon tomato paste

½ teaspoon chili powder

¼ teaspoon ground cumin

¼ teaspoon kosher salt

¼ teaspoon freshly ground black pepper

¼ pound ground beef

¼ cup corn kernels, fresh, frozen, or drained canned

1 tablespoon chopped black olives

METHOD

1. *To make the filling:* In a jumbo mug, combine 1 tablespoon of the butter, the onion, and tomato and microwave for 1 to 2 minutes until the vegetables are tender. Stir in the tomato paste, chili powder, cumin, salt, pepper, and beef and mix well. Fold in the corn and olives, then microwave again until the meat is cooked through, 3 to 4 minutes. Set aside.

2. *To make the topping:* In a separate mug, combine the cornmeal, salt, cumin, water, and oil and stir to make a batter. Fold in the cheese, then pour the batter on top of the mug with the filling. Microwave again for 1 to 2 minutes until the batter is risen and firm. Serve immediately with a dollop of sour cream.

Topping

¼ cup cornmeal

Pinch of kosher salt

Pinch of ground cumin, plus more for garnish

¼ cup cold water

1 teaspoon vegetable oil

2 tablespoons grated cheddar cheese

Sour cream, for serving

• VARIATIONS •

FRITO PIE: Another Tex-Mex creation, the Frito pie typically involves chili or barbecued meat poured over a pile of corn chips. Here, you can simply use them to replace the second mug of corn bread batter. Omit the cornmeal, salt, cumin, water, and oil. Instead, fold in ½ cup of corn chips and the cheese into the mug of meat filling and cook for another minute to warm through.

5

birds +
fish

Some of the recipes in this chapter call for the poultry and fish to be precooked. This not only speeds up the process, but also lets you make some interesting meals out of your leftovers. (You can also use canned meats, which are readily available and perfectly fine for these recipes.) If, however, you do not have leftover meat or canned meats on hand, cooking poultry and fish from scratch in the microwave is not difficult. It takes only 2 to 3 minutes for a mug-size serving. A little fat added to the mug helps conduct the heat and retain moisture.

For $1/2$ cup of poultry or fish, add 1 tablespoon of olive oil and heat for 1 minute. Stop, stir, then heat for another minute. Stir again, and continue that process until the meat is fully cooked.

Arroz con Pollo

Every Spanish-speaking country has a unique variation of this dish. Here, I included achiote paste, which is a common ingredient in the Yucatan. Feel free to leave it out, or vary the seasonings to your taste—just don't leave out the arroz or the pollo.

INGREDIENTS

1 tablespoon olive oil

¼ teaspoon achiote paste

¼ cup minced yellow onion

½ garlic clove, minced

½ small tomato, chopped

¼ cup long-grain rice

½ cup water

2 to 3 pimiento-stuffed green olives, chopped

½ serrano or jalapeño chile, seeded and minced

¼ teaspoon ground cumin

Pinch of ground cloves

¼ cup roasted red bell peppers

1 tablespoon minced fresh cilantro leaves

2 tablespoons peas, fresh or frozen

½ cup shredded cooked chicken meat

¼ teaspoon kosher salt

¼ teaspoon freshly ground black pepper

METHOD

1. In a jumbo mug, combine the oil, achiote paste, onion, and garlic. Microwave for 1 to 2 minutes until the onion is tender. Add the tomato, rice, and water, cover loosely, and microwave for 2 to 3 minutes. Set aside for 20 minutes to allow the rice to absorb the liquid, then microwave again for 3 to 5 minutes until the rice is tender.

2. Drain any excess liquid from the rice, then add the olives, chile, cumin, cloves, roasted bell peppers, cilantro, peas, chicken, salt, and black pepper. Stir to mix thoroughly and microwave for another 1 to 2 minutes until heated through. Serve immediately.

Chicken Chilaquiles

Chilaquiles is a classic peasant dish from South of the Border. Here in The States it is sometimes called Mexican lasagna. There are as many variations as there are families. This recipe uses chips, but it can just as easily be made with torn tortillas. Anything goes—as long as you don't skimp on the cheese.

INGREDIENTS

1 tablespoon olive oil

1 small jalapeño chile, seeded and diced

1 scallion, minced

½ garlic clove, minced

¼ cup minced fresh cilantro

1 small tomato, diced

¼ teaspoon ground cumin

Dash of Tabasco sauce

¼ teaspoon kosher salt

¼ teaspoon freshly ground black pepper

8 to 10 tortilla chips

½ cup shredded cooked chicken meat

¼ cup sour cream

¼ cup grated cheddar cheese

1 tablespoon salsa or pico de gallo

METHOD

1. In a large mug, combine the oil, jalapeño, scallion, and garlic and microwave for 1 to 2 minutes until the vegetables are tender. Stir in the cilantro, tomato, cumin, Tabasco, salt, and pepper and mix well.

2. In a jumbo mug, layer 1 to 2 chips, 2 to 3 pieces of chicken, 1 tablespoon of sour cream, 1 tablespoon of the vegetable mixture, and 1 tablespoon of the grated cheese. Repeat until all the ingredients are used. Finish with a tablespoon of salsa, and microwave for 1 to 2 minutes until heated through. Serve immediately.

(continued)

Chicken Chilaquiles (continued)

• VARIATIONS •

AVOCADO: Top your creation with guacamole, or add a layer of sliced ripe avocado.

VEGETARIAN: This isn't hard. Just leave out the chicken! You can add beans in their place if you'd like to increase your protein intake.

READY-MADE SAUCE: Canned enchilada sauce can really speed up this already speedy meal. Use it in place of the preparation in the first step, layering it with the chips, meat, sour cream, and cheese.

CHEESE OPTIONS: Try this with the traditional Mexican cotija, or something similar, like ricotta or feta. It will be less gooey, but no less delicious.

Kung Pao Chicken

A standard menu item in American Chinese restaurants, it originally hails from the Sichuan Province of China, where they take their heat seriously. You can increase or decrease the spice here as much as you like. It's your mug!

INGREDIENTS

1 teaspoon vegetable oil

¼ teaspoon sesame oil

1 garlic clove, minced

¼ teaspoon peeled and grated fresh ginger

1 scallion, chopped

1 small chicken breast, sliced into bite-size pieces

1 dried red chile, minced, or ½ teaspoon hot red chile flakes

Pinch of cracked Sichuan peppercorns

½ teaspoon cornstarch

1 teaspoon soy sauce

1 teaspoon rice wine or rice vinegar

½ teaspoon honey

1 tablespoon minced fresh cilantro

1 tablespoon chopped peanuts

METHOD

1. In a jumbo mug, combine the vegetable oil, sesame oil, garlic, and ginger and microwave for 30 to 60 seconds until the garlic is tender. Stir in the scallion, chicken, chile, and Sichuan pepper and microwave for 2 to 3 minutes, stirring every minute, until the chicken is cooked through.

2. In a separate mug, stir together the cornstarch, soy sauce, rice wine, and honey. Pour into the chicken mug, and stir to coat evenly. Microwave for another 30 to 60 seconds to warm through. Stir in the cilantro and peanuts and serve immediately.

Chicken Satay

Satay is originally an Indonesian dish of skewered meats in a savory peanut sauce. There are similar versions throughout Asia, Africa, and the Middle East, but in the United States it is usually associated with Thai cuisine. Here, I have omitted the satay sticks, but if you close your eyes, you can still pretend you are in Angkor.

INGREDIENTS

1 teaspoon peanut or vegetable oil

¼ teaspoon sesame oil

½ garlic clove, minced

1 small chicken breast, sliced into bite-size pieces

1 tablespoon peanut butter

1 teaspoon fresh lime juice

½ teaspoon soy sauce

Dash of sriracha sauce

1 scallion, minced

1 tablespoon chopped fresh cilantro

¼ cup finely chopped peanuts

METHOD

In a large mug, combine the peanut oil, sesame oil, garlic, and chicken and stir to coat. Microwave for 2 to 3 minutes until the chicken is half-cooked. Add the peanut butter, lime juice, soy sauce, sriracha, and scallion. Microwave again for another 1 to 2 minutes until the chicken is completely cooked. Serve immediately topped with the chopped cilantro and peanuts.

• VARIATIONS •

SWEETEN IT UP: For a fruiter take on this classic, try adding a sliced banana or plantain, and a drizzle of coconut milk.

VEGETARIAN: This peanut sauce works remarkably well with sweet potatoes, parsnips, and even tofu. Just replace the meat with your favorite vegetarian alternative.

Blackened Catfish
with Cajun Remoulade

MAKES 1 MUG

Blackening takes place on a very hot grill or pan. We are using neither of those things here, but that doesn't mean we can't approximate this NOLA specialty.

INGREDIENTS

Remoulade Sauce

2 tablespoons mayonnaise

¼ teaspoon capers

¼ teaspoon minced gherkins or cornichons

1 teaspoon minced fresh flat-leaf parsley

Dash of Tabasco sauce

Catfish

One 3- to 4-ounce catfish fillet

1 tablespoon olive oil

¼ teaspoon kosher salt

¼ teaspoon freshly ground black pepper

⅛ teaspoon cayenne pepper

⅛ teaspoon garlic powder

¼ teaspoon onion powder

½ teaspoon dried thyme

METHOD

1. To make the remoulade sauce: In a small mug, combine the mayonnaise, capers, gherkins, parsley, and Tabasco. Stir to combine, and set the sauce aside in the fridge.

2. To prepare the catfish: In a large mug, combine the oil, salt, pepper, cayenne, garlic powder, onion powder, and thyme. Microwave for 30 to 60 seconds to warm through. Add the catfish, sliced into bite-sized pieces; stir to coat with the spiced oil, then microwave for 1 to 2 minutes until the fish is cooked through. Serve immediately, topped with remoulade sauce.

Shrimp Scampi

Another simple and delicious take on seafood, this dish is commonly found smothering a pile of pasta. With or without the side of starch, it is "shrimp-a-licious."

INGREDIENTS

1 tablespoon unsalted butter

1 scallion, chopped

2 garlic cloves, minced

Finely grated zest and juice of ½ lemon

1 tablespoon minced fresh flat-leaf parsley

¼ cup white wine

Pinch of kosher salt

Pinch of freshly ground black pepper

¼ pound medium shrimp, peeled and deveined

Crusty French bread, for serving

METHOD

1. In a large mug, combine the butter, scallion, and garlic and microwave for 30 to 60 seconds until the vegetables are tender. Stir in the lemon zest and juice, parsley, wine, salt, and pepper. Add the shrimp, toss to coat, and microwave for 2 to 3 minutes, stirring every minute, until the shrimp are pink. Serve immediately with crusty French bread.

Coconut Shrimp

MAKES 1 MUG

This dish was the first seafood I could get my kids to eat. Crispy, crunchy, and a little exotic, it will woo even the most persnickety eater.

INGREDIENTS

1 tablespoon olive oil

1 garlic clove

¼ cup shredded coconut (unsweetened is best)

2 tablespoons panko or regular bread crumbs

½ teaspoon dried thyme

¼ teaspoon kosher salt

¼ teaspoon freshly ground black pepper

¼ pound medium shrimp, peeled and deveined

METHOD

1. In a jumbo mug, combine the oil, garlic, coconut, bread crumbs, and thyme. Mix thoroughly and microwave for 30 seconds to warm through. Add the shrimp, toss to coat, and microwave for another 2 to 3 minutes, stirring once or twice, until the shrimp are cooked. Serve immediately.

• VARIATIONS •

SPICE IT UP: Add a dash or two of Tabasco, sriracha, or a tablespoon of chopped jalapeño or canned green chiles.

Jerk Chicken and Rice

MAKES 1 MUG

Though traditionally applied to goat or lamb, today you can find jerk seasoning enhancing seafood, beef, and even tofu. Anyway it's used, this Jamaican spice blend is a hallmark of island cuisine.

INGREDIENTS

1 tablespoon olive oil

2 tablespoons jerk seasoning (store-bought, or homemade; see sidebar)

¼ cup minced yellow onion

2 tablespoons seeded and minced green bell pepper

½ garlic clove, minced

¼ cup long-grain rice

½ cup water

½ serrano or jalapeño chile, seeded and minced

1 tablespoon minced fresh cilantro leaves

½ cup shredded cooked chicken meat

¼ teaspoon kosher salt

¼ teaspoon freshly ground black pepper

Lime wedge, for squeezing

METHOD

1. In a jumbo mug, combine the oil, jerk seasoning, onion, bell pepper, and garlic. Microwave for 1 to 2 minutes until the vegetables are tender. Add the rice and water, cover loosely, and microwave for 2 to 3 minutes. Set aside for 20 minutes to allow the rice to absorb the liquid, then microwave again for 3 to 5 minutes until the rice is tender.

2. Drain any excess water from the rice. Add the jalapeños, cilantro, chicken, salt, and black pepper to the rice and stir to mix thoroughly. Microwave for another 1 to 2 minutes to heat through. Serve immediately topped with a squeeze of lime juice, and a dollop of plain yogurt or sour cream, if desired.

HOMEMADE JERK SEASONING

If you can't find jerk in your market (there are plenty of jerks in mine) you can make your own! It's easy, Man.

INGREDIENTS

2 tablespoon dried thyme

1 tablespoon ground allspice

1 tablespoon brown sugar

1 teaspoon freshly ground black pepper

1 teaspoon ground cinnamon

1 teaspoon freshly grated nutmeg

1 teaspoon ground ginger

METHOD

Mix all the ingredients together and store in an airtight container.

• VARIATIONS •

WHOLE SPICES: If you have the time and the inclination, use whole spices rather than ground ones. Toast each in a dry skillet until fragrant, then grind them together in a coffee mill.

Poached Salmon with Dill

Healthy and delicious, salmon is one of the easiest fish to prepare. I like mine on the rare side, but you can cook yours as long as you like. Beware, though—overcooking leads to a rubbery texture.

INGREDIENTS

1 tablespoon olive oil

1 scallion, minced

2 tablespoons minced fresh dill, or 1 teaspoon dried dill weed

Pinch of kosher salt

Pinch of freshly ground black pepper

One 4- to 5-ounce salmon fillet

2 tablespoons white wine

1 slice of lemon, or 1 tablespoon fresh lemon juice

Sour cream or plain yogurt, for serving

METHOD

1. In a small mug, combine the oil, scallion, dill, salt, and pepper. Mix well and set aside.

2. Cut the salmon into 2 to 3 pieces that will fit into a large mug. Layer the salmon pieces in the large mug with the dill mixture, finishing with dill on top. Pour the wine over the salmon, place the lemon slice on top, and cover the mug loosely with plastic wrap. Microwave for 2 to 3 minutes until the salmon is cooked thorough. Serve immediately with a dollop of sour cream or plain yogurt.

Crab Cake

Though not technically a crab cake, this recipe is still a mug full of crustaceous delight.

INGREDIENTS

1 tablespoon olive oil

¼ cup minced yellow onion

1 tablespoon seeded and minced red or green bell pepper

½ garlic clove

2 tablespoons mayonnaise

Dash of Dijon mustard

½ teaspoon Old Bay seasoning

½ teaspoon fresh lemon juice

¼ teaspoon kosher salt

¼ teaspoon freshly ground black pepper

¼ cup crushed saltine crackers or bread crumbs

½ cup crabmeat, fresh, frozen, or canned

Sour cream, tartar sauce, or remoulade sauce, for serving

METHOD

1. In a large mug, combine the oil, onion, bell pepper, and garlic and microwave for 1 to 2 minutes until the vegetables are tender. Stir in the mayonnaise, mustard, Old Bay, lemon juice, salt, and black pepper and mix thoroughly. Stir in the cracker crumbs and crabmeat, and mix until well coated.

2. Divide the mixture between two mugs, and press it down to the bottom to form patties. Microwave each for 1 to 2 minutes until firm and sizzling. Turn the patties out onto a plate, and serve immediately with a dollop of sour cream, tartar sauce, or remoulade sauce (see Blackened Catfish, Cajun Remoulade recipe, page 96)

• VARIATIONS •

FISH OPTIONS: Recipes like this were historically used to finish up leftovers, because any portion of protein was precious. You can use any seafood you have on hand.

SPICY CAKES: Add a teaspoon of Cajun seasoning, a dash or two of Tabasco or sriracha sauce, or a tablespoon of chopped jalapeño or canned green chiles.

Turkey Tetrazzini

Luisa Tetrazzini was an Italian opera star who inspired a number of hotel chefs at the turn of the twentieth century, including those at the Palace Hotel in San Francisco, and the Knickerbocker Hotel in New York, both of which claim to have originated this simple but delicious recipe.

INGREDIENTS

½ cup spaghetti noodles, broken into 1- to 2-inch pieces

1 tablespoon olive oil

¼ cup minced yellow onion

2 tablespoons seeded and chopped red bell pepper

1 garlic clove, minced

3 to 4 cremini or white button mushrooms, chopped

1 teaspoon fresh thyme leaves, or ¼ teaspoon dried thyme

1 cup shredded cooked turkey

½ cup turkey broth, chicken broth, or water

½ cup heavy cream

¼ teaspoon kosher salt

¼ teaspoon freshly ground black pepper

1 tablespoon minced fresh flat-leaf parsley

METHOD

1. In a large mug, combine the spaghetti with enough water to cover. Cover loosely with plastic and microwave for 2 to 3 minutes. Set aside for 20 minutes to absorb the water, then microwave again for 3 to 5 minutes until tender.

2. In a large mug, combine the oil, onion, bell pepper, garlic, mushrooms, and thyme. Microwave for 1 to 2 minutes until the onion is tender. Drain the excess water from the spaghetti, add the spaghetti to the jumbo mug, and stir to combine. Add the turkey, broth, cream, salt, and black pepper and stir to mix thoroughly. Microwave for another 1 to 2 minutes until heated through. Stir in the parsley and the grated Parmesan cheese, if desired, and serve immediately.

6

pasta

The following recipes call for cooked pasta, but it's up to you to choose the cooking method that best suits your circumstances. The recipes work well with whichever type of pasta you prefer. I usually use whole wheat, but there are a number of grains used to make pasta these days, including rice, and quinoa. Cooking times will vary depending on the grain and the manufacturer, so a little experimentation may be in order.

Microwaving pasta is not difficult, but it can be messy. The process involves, as you may know, boiling water—something that the microwave excels at. But it is nearly impossible to regulate a microwave's heat. When pasta is cooked in a pot on the stovetop, and the water starts to boil over, you can easily turn the heat down. But if the water starts to boil over in a microwave, you have to stop and regroup. This is, however, not an insurmountable problem. There are three remedies to the boiling-over water problem.

1. Boil the pasta in a very large microwavable container. It needs to be large enough to hold 2 cups of water, with ample room to boil up, but not over. For the mug recipes in this chapter you will need at least a quart-sized container. The finished pasta can then be drained, and added to the mug along with the other ingredients in your recipe.

Combine ¼ cup pasta with 2 cups of water in a large, quart-sized container. Microwave for 8 to 10 minutes, or until the pasta is tender. Drain and continue with recipe as directed.

2. Let partially cooked pasta sit in the mug and soften for 30 minutes, then finish cooking and complete the recipe. This takes longer (not something microwave cooks are always willing do), but if you have only a microwave and limited space, this is the most viable option.

In a jumbo mug, combine ¼ cup pasta with 2 cups of water. Cover loosely with plastic wrap and microwave for 2 minutes. Set it aside, covered, for 30 minutes to soften. (I usually just leave it in the microwave oven.) After the 30 minutes, microwave again for another 2 minutes. It should cook until it starts to boil up, which may take a little more or less than 2 minutes, depending on your oven. Keep an eye on it. Then drain the pasta and proceed with the recipe as written. I would be remiss if I didn't mention that this method takes longer than simply boiling pasta on the stovetop, which leads me to option 3 . . .

3. If you are not limited to a microwave, you might consider breaking out the pots and pans. Cook a large batch of pasta on the stovetop, then freeze it, fully cooked, in small, mug-size batches. This speeds up your mug preparation time, and helps keep your portions in check.

Carbonara Shells

Carbone is the Italian word for "coal," and this dish is thought to have been named in honor of Italian coal miners because it contains ingredients that could be easily transported without refrigeration to work in the mines. Then again, some people think it was so named because the black pepper in this white sauce looks a lot like ash. That's the great thing about culinary history—it's always a little mysterious.

INGREDIENTS

¼ cup diced pancetta, or 1 slice bacon, diced

¼ cup heavy cream

1 large egg

2 tablespoons grated Parmesan cheese

¼ teaspoon kosher salt

¼ teaspoon freshly ground black pepper

1 cup cooked small pasta shells (conchiglie)

1 tablespoon minced fresh flat-leaf parsley

METHOD

In a large mug, microwave the pancetta for 30 to 60 seconds until the pancetta is cooked and the fat has rendered. Stir in the cream, egg, cheese, salt, and pepper and beat with a fork until frothy. Add the cooked pasta shells and microwave for another 30 to 60 seconds until the sauce has warmed through and thickened. Serve immediately, topped with the parsley.

Farfalle with Garlic and Clams

MAKES 1 MUG

Farfalla is the Italian word for "butterfly," but you might know this pasta by its pseudonym, "bowtie."

INGREDIENTS

1 slice bacon, diced

1 garlic clove, minced

1 scallion, chopped

¼ cup canned chopped clams with their juices (about ½ small can)

¼ cup heavy cream

¼ teaspoon kosher salt

¼ teaspoon freshly ground black pepper

1 cup cooked pasta bowties (farfalle)

1 tablespoon minced fresh flat-leaf parsley

1 tablespoon grated Parmesan cheese

METHOD

In a large mug, microwave the bacon, garlic, and scallion for 1 to 2 minutes until the bacon is cooked through and the fat has rendered. Pour off all but 1 tablespoon of the fat. Stir in the clams, cream, salt, and pepper. Add the farfalle and microwave for another 30 to 60 seconds until the sauce is heated through. Serve immediately, topped with the parsley and grated cheese.

Greek Orzo with Feta and Olives

MAKES 1 MUG

Orzo is Italian for "barley," which is a reference to the size of this pasta. It is also sometimes called *risoni*, meaning "big rice," which is a better description. Don't be limited by its Italian name, though. This pasta shape is popular throughout the Mediterranean region.

INGREDIENTS

1 tablespoon olive oil

¼ cup diced red onion

½ garlic clove, minced

1 tablespoon fresh oregano (or ½ teaspoon dried)

½ small tomato, diced

4 to 5 kalamata olives, pitted and chopped

1 teaspoon red wine vinegar or fresh lemon juice

¼ teaspoon kosher salt

¼ teaspoon freshly ground black pepper

1 cup cooked orzo

¼ cup crumbled feta cheese

1 teaspoon minced fresh mint

METHOD

In a large mug, combine the oil, onion, garlic, oregano, and tomato. Microwave for 1 to 2 minutes until the vegetables are tender. Stir in the olives, vinegar, salt, and pepper and microwave for another 30 to 60 seconds to warm through. Add the orzo and feta, and serve immediately, topped with the mint.

Lasagna

Most microwave lasagna recipes are noodle-free, layering ready-made sauce, pepperoni, and cheese in a mug and heating until the cheese has melted. But lasagna with no noodles is, to me, wholly unsatisfying. And I am not a fan of ready-made sauce. If you are similarly snooty, you will appreciate this rendition. If you are less pretentious, I have included the more common technique in the variations.

INGREDIENTS

1 teaspoon olive oil

½ garlic clove, minced

3 to 4 mushrooms, sliced

1 tablespoon fresh oregano (or ½ teaspoon dried)

1 large tomato, finely chopped (or 1 cup canned crushed tomato)

¼ teaspoon kosher salt

¼ teaspoon freshly ground black pepper

2 strips lasagna noodles, broken into 2-inch lengths and partially cooked

¼ cup ricotta cheese

3 to 4 slices fresh mozzarella

1 tablespoon grated Parmesan cheese

1 tablespoon minced fresh basil

METHOD

1. In a large mug, combine the oil, garlic, mushrooms, oregano, tomato, salt, and pepper.

Microwave for 1 to 2 minutes until the vegetables are tender. Set the tomato sauce aside.

2. In a second large mug, layer the lasagna in the following order: tomato sauce, noodles, ricotta, mozzarella. Repeat this layering, finishing with sauce and a sprinkling of Parmesan cheese. Microwave for 30 to 60 seconds to heat through and melt the cheese. Serve immediately, topped with the basil.

(continued)

Lasagna (continued)

• VARIATIONS •

ITALIAN SAUSAGE: If you like meaty lasagna, cook a link of Italian sausage in a separate mug. Remove the casing, crumble the meat, and put in a mug with 2 to 3 tablespoons of water. Microwave for 2 to 3 minutes until cooked through, then drain off the liquid. Layer the cooked sausage in with tomato sauce.

SPINACH: A few leaves of fresh spinach layered in with the cheese adds color, nutrition, and a fresh, bright flavor.

EGGPLANT: Eggplant is a mainstay of vegetarian lasagna because of its meaty texture. Put ¼ cup of diced eggplant in a mug with a pinch of salt and 2 to 3 tablespoons of water. Microwave for 2 to 3 minutes until tender, then drain off the liquid, and layer the eggplant with the tomato sauce.

NO PASTA: Do your layering as written, but omit the pasta. You can add any precooked ingredients you like, including spinach or eggplant, as above, or any precooked meat, like pepperoni. You can also skip the first step and use a can of ready-made tomato sauce.

Kugel

This baked pasta casserole was originally a hearty Ashkenazi Jewish specialty. It is not uncommon to see variations made with potato, bread, or matzo instead of noodles, and it can land anywhere on the scale from sweet to savory. This recipe is on the sweeter side.

INGREDIENTS

2 tablespoons golden or dark raisins

1 large egg

2 tablespoons whole milk

1 tablespoon brown sugar

¼ teaspoon pure vanilla extract

¼ cup ricotta or cottage cheese

1 tablespoon unsalted butter

Pinch of kosher salt

Pinch of ground cinnamon

Pinch of freshly grated nutmeg

1 cup cooked egg noodles

METHOD

1. Put the raisins in a mug and cover with water. Microwave for 1 minute, then set aside to plump.

2. In a separate large mug, whisk together the egg, milk, sugar, and vanilla with a fork until frothy. Stir in the ricotta, butter, salt, cinnamon, and nutmeg. Fold in the egg noodles and drained raisins. Microwave for 30 to 60 seconds to warm through. Serve immediately.

• VARIATIONS •

APPLE: A popular variation, to make it add ¼ cup of applesauce with the ricotta. Or, precook a fresh apple. Put 1 small, peeled, cored, and grated apple in a mug, cover with water, and microwave for 2 to 3 minutes until tender. Drain and add with the ricotta.

Nuked Ziti

Ziti is the tube-shaped pasta with straight ends. It is traditionally long, like spaghetti, but is seen more often in the United States cut short, like penne, but without the pointed ends. Baked ziti has always been one of my all-time favorite easy meals. Making it in a mug is even easier.

INGREDIENTS

1 cup Italian sausage, casing removed, meat crumbled

1 garlic clove, minced

3 to 4 mushrooms, sliced

1 tablespoon dried Italian seasoning

¼ teaspoon kosher salt

¼ teaspoon freshly ground black pepper

1 large tomato, finely chopped (or 1 cup canned crushed tomato)

¼ cup ricotta cheese

1 cup cooked whole wheat ziti or penne

1 tablespoon grated mozzarella cheese

1 tablespoon grated Parmesan cheese

METHOD

In a large mug, combine the sausage, garlic, mushrooms, and Italian seasoning. Microwave for 2 to 3 minutes until the meat is cooked through and the vegetables are tender. Pour off all but 1 tablespoon of the fat. Add the salt, pepper, tomato, ricotta, and ziti and mix thoroughly. Top with the mozzarella and microwave for 30 to 60 seconds to warm through and melt the cheese. Serve immediately, topped with the Parmesan cheese.

Pecorino Pesto Penne

Pecorino Romano is a hard Italian cheese, similar to Parmesan, but made from the milk of sheep rather than cows. As a result, its taste is a bit sharper and saltier. That said, you can easily use Parmesan instead. When cooking in mugs, it pays to be flexible.

INGREDIENTS

1 cup cooked penne

¼ cup pesto sauce, store-bought or mug-made (see page 122)

2 tablespoons grated pecorino Romano cheese

¼ teaspoon kosher salt

¼ teaspoon freshly ground black pepper

METHOD

In a large mug, combine the pasta, pesto, and pecorino. Microwave for 1 to 2 minutes to warm through. Add salt and pepper, to taste. Serve immediately.

MUG PESTO

MAKES ½ – ¾ CUP PESTO

You can find ready-made pesto in practically every store. But if you have the time and inclination, it is supereasy to make at home in large batches or little mugs.

INGREDIENTS

2 tablespoons olive oil

2 garlic cloves, minced

2 tablespoons walnuts, pecans, or pine nuts, minced

½ teaspoon kosher salt

2 cups minced fresh basil leaves

¼ cup grated Parmesan cheese

METHOD

In a large mug, combine the oil, garlic, and nuts. Microwave for 30 to 60 seconds until the garlic is tender. Add the salt and basil, and, using the handle of a wooden spoon, stir and crush the mixture into a rough paste. Mix in the Parmesan, and add additional oil as needed to reach a smooth, spreadable consistency. Use the pesto right away, or store in the refrigerator for a week. For longer storage, freeze in an airtight container.

Truffle Mac

Truffle oil is superfancy. Usually, however, it is used with too heavy a hand. Its umami essence can easily overpower every other ingredient in a dish. For that reason, it needs to be used extremely sparingly. This also makes the big price of those tiny bottles easier to come to terms with.

INGREDIENTS

1 teaspoon unsalted butter

½ garlic clove

2 to 3 cremini or white button mushrooms, minced

½ cup Gruyère cheese

¼ cup ricotta cheese

1 scant drop truffle oil

Pinch of kosher salt

Pinch of freshly ground black pepper

1 cup cooked macaroni

METHOD

In a large mug, combine the butter, garlic, and mushrooms. Microwave for 1 to 2 minutes until the vegetables are tender. Add the Gruyère, ricotta, truffle oil, salt, and pepper and mix well. Fold in the cooked macaroni and stir well, Microwave for another 30 to 60 seconds until the cheese has melted. Serve immediately.

Orecchiette Alfredo

MAKES 1 MUG

The name of this pasta comes from the Italian *orecchio*, which means "ear." I guess it looks like a tiny ear, but I prefer to think of it as a little bowl. This shape is perfect for capturing thick sauces—each little bowl carries a tiny portion of the sauce.

INGREDIENTS

1 tablespoon unsalted butter

½ garlic clove, minced

½ cup heavy cream

¼ cup grated Parmesan cheese

¼ teaspoon kosher salt

¼ teaspoon freshly ground black pepper

1 cup cooked orecchiette or small pasta shells

1 tablespoon minced fresh flat-leaf parsley

METHOD

In a large mug, microwave the butter and garlic for 30 to 60 until the butter has melted. Stir in the cream, Parmesan, salt, and pepper and mix well, then stir in the cooked pasta. Microwave for another 30 to 60 seconds until the sauce is heated through. Serve immediately, topped with the parsley.

Tuna Noodles

Tuna noodle casserole is usually bound with a roux-based béchamel or velouté sauce, but the mug version doesn't really need binding. The result is less heavy, but no less satisfying.

INGREDIENTS

1 tablespoon unsalted butter

1 scallion, chopped

2 to 3 cremini or white button mushrooms

¼ cup canned tuna with its oil or water (about ½ small can)

2 tablespoons heavy cream

2 tablespoons peas, fresh or frozen

¼ teaspoon kosher salt

¼ teaspoon freshly ground black pepper

1 cup cooked egg noodles or small pasta shells

1 tablespoon minced fresh flat-leaf parsley

3 to 4 potato chips, crushed

METHOD

In a jumbo mug, microwave the butter, scallion, and mushrooms for 30 to 60 seconds until the vegetables are tender. Stir in the tuna, cream, peas, salt, and pepper. Fold in the cooked noodles and microwave for another 30 to 60 seconds until the sauce is heated through. Serve immediately, topped with the parsley and crushed potato chips.

White Cheddar Macaroni

Cheddar cheese was originally yellow because the dairy cows ate grass high in beta-carotene. In the colder months, when a diet of hay dramatically lightened the cheese's color, cheese makers started adding artificially coloring agents, most notably the annatto seed. Though white cheddar is nothing more than cheese in its natural state, it often has a sharper flavor. As with all of my recipes, you should feel free to make this with whatever cheddar you have in the cheese drawer.

INGREDIENTS

½ cup grated white cheddar cheese

¼ cup whole milk

¼ teaspoon Dijon mustard

1 teaspoon unsalted butter

¼ teaspoon kosher salt

¼ teaspoon freshly ground black pepper

1 cup cooked macaroni

2 to 3 crumbled crackers or crushed potato chips

METHOD

Put the cheese, milk, mustard, butter, salt, and pepper in a large mug. Stir well, then microwave for 1 to 2 minutes until the cheese has melted. Fold in the cooked macaroni and microwave for another 30 seconds to warm through. Serve immediately, topped with the crumbled crackers.

• VARIATIONS •

VEGGIE MAC: This dish can be nutritionally and deliciously enhanced with ¼ cup of chopped broccoli, green beans, peas, asparagus, sautéed mushrooms, onions, or any leftover vegetables you might have on hand.

MEATY MAC: The addition of ¼ cup diced ham, sausage, or other precooked meat makes this mug a extra-hardy meal.

Pasta Puttanesca

If you believe the stories, this salty dish was popularized by Italian ladies of the night, who made this quick dish from readily available pantry ingredients. I think it could just as easily be called "bachelor pasta."

INGREDIENTS

1 tablespoon olive oil

1 garlic clove, minced

1 anchovy fillets, roughly chopped

2 to 3 kalamata olives, pitted and roughly chopped

½ teaspoon capers

1 large tomato, finely chopped, or 1 cup canned crushed tomatoes

Pinch of freshly ground black pepper

1 cup cooked whole wheat spaghetti (broken into 2 to 3 inch pieces before cooking)

1 tablespoon chopped fresh basil leaves

METHOD

In a large mug, combine the oil, garlic, and anchovies and microwave for 30 to 60 seconds until the garlic is tender. Add the olives, capers, tomato, and pepper and mix well. Fold in the cooked pasta and microwave for another 1 to 2 minutes to heat through. Serve immediately, topped with the basil.

veggies + grains

Grains can be cooked in the microwave, but they take a while. For this reason, the recipes here call for the grains to be precooked. This makes them the perfect vehicle for leftovers. However you can certainly cook the grains from scratch in the microwave. The process is similar to that for pasta, in that it takes longer than most microwaving. If possible, I prefer to cook grains in larger batches—either in the microwave or on a traditional stovetop—and then store them in single-serve portions in the freezer. This makes mug meals fast and easy.

To precook grains in the microwave, choose a microwave container with plenty of headroom to prevent boil-overs. Cover ¼ cup of grain with 1 cup of water, and microwave for 2 minutes. Let stand for 30–40 minutes, then microwave again for 2 to 3 minutes, until tender. Drain off water before adding to recipe.

Vegetables cook fast—usually within 1 or 2 minutes. That should provide you ample incentive to reach for these recipes instead of that bag of chips when you're infected with the snack bug.

Barley and Bacon

MAKES 1 MUG

Barley needs a better publicist. Its hearty, chewy texture is just as hip as quinoa and spelt.

INGREDIENTS

1 slice bacon, diced

1 scallion, chopped

Finely grated zest and juice of 1 orange

¼ teaspoon kosher salt

¼ teaspoon freshly ground black pepper

1 tablespoon minced fresh flat-leaf parsley

¼ cup barley, cooked

METHOD

In a large mug, combine the bacon and scallion and microwave for 1 to 2 minutes until the bacon is crisp and the fat has rendered. Pour off all but 1 tablespoon of the fat. Add the orange zest and juice, salt, pepper, parsley, and cooked barley. Microwave for another 1 to 2 minutes to warm through. Serve immediately.

> ### • VARIATIONS •
>
> **GRAIN OPTIONS:** This recipe is also delightful when made with, spelt, kamut, quinoa, millet, or brown rice.

Brown Butter Green Beans

MAKES 1 MUG

This is my favorite sauce to make, because it is really easy, and really delicious. After you make this, try it on every vegetable you can imagine.

INGREDIENTS

1 cup green beans, cut into 2-inch lengths

2 tablespoons unsalted butter

Pinch of kosher salt

Pinch of freshly ground black pepper

METHOD

1. Put the beans in a large mug and cover with water. Cover loosely with plastic wrap and microwave for 1 to 2 minutes until bright green and tender. Drain the beans.

2. Put the butter in a second mug and microwave for 1 to 2 minutes until the butter has melted and begun to brown. Add the salt, pepper, and beans, and toss to coat. Microwave again for another minute to warm through. Serve immediately.

> • VARIATIONS •
>
> **VEGGIE OPTIONS:** Try this recipe with fava beans, asparagus, broccoli, peas, and even Brussels sprouts.
>
> **HERBY:** All vegetables benefit from a dose of an herb. Add 2 tablespoons of chopped fresh flat-leaf parsley, chervil, thyme, basil, or chives. Or use ½ teaspoon of dried herbs, like my favorite, herbes de Provence.
>
> **DRIED BEANS:** Brown butter is a lovely finish to simple legumes, too. Replace the green beans with an equal amount of canned white, fava, or garbanzo beans.

Collard Greens and Ham Hocks

Traditionally, collard greens were cooked for a long period of time. After an hour or more, the resulting wilted, olive-green mush took on the flavors of the smoked meat, vinegar, and chiles, with very little vegetable flavor remaining. Now we know that such prolonged cooking greatly reduces a vegetable's nutritional value. We have also learned to appreciate a vegetable's natural flavor. This recipe highlights the greens, and uses additional ingredients to enhance, rather than mask, their natural goodness.

INGREDIENTS

1 tablespoon unsalted butter

¼ cup chopped yellow onion

Dash of Tabasco sauce

1 teaspoon fresh lemon juice

¼ cup diced smoked ham hock meat, or other smoked ham

2 cups washed and chopped collard greens

¼ teaspoon kosher salt

¼ teaspoon freshly ground black pepper

METHOD

In a large mug, combine the butter, onion, Tabasco, lemon juice, and ham. Microwave for 1 to 2 minutes until the butter has melted. Add the collard greens, salt, and pepper and toss to coat. Microwave for another 1 to 2 minutes, stopping intermittently to stir, until the collard greens have wilted. Serve immediately.

• VARIATIONS •

BACON GREENS: Replace the butter with 1 slice of diced bacon. Cook until the bacon is crisp, and the fat has rendered. Pour off all but 1 tablespoon of the fat, and continue with the recipe as written.

OTHER GREENS: This dish works well with a number of leafy greens, including kale, turnip greens, Swiss chard, and spinach.

Creamed Spinach

MAKES 1 MUG

This recipe is a classic side dish in traditional steak houses. But you certainly don't need a steak to enjoy it.

INGREDIENTS

1 tablespoon unsalted butter

1 scallion

1 tablespoon whole milk

2 tablespoons cream cheese

¼ teaspoon kosher salt

¼ teaspoon freshly ground black pepper

Pinch of freshly grated nutmeg

3 cups fresh spinach, roughly chopped

METHOD

In a jumbo mug, combine the butter, scallion, milk, cream cheese, salt, pepper, and nutmeg. Microwave for 1 to 2 minutes, stirring intermittently, until the butter has melted and the cheese has softened. Mix into a smooth sauce, then add the spinach and toss to coat. Microwave for another 1 to 2 minutes, stopping intermittently to stir, until the spinach has wilted. Serve immediately.

Candied Sweet Potatoes

Sometimes a holiday meal is good for the soul. Even in June. This recipe offers you a taste of autumn at a moment's notice.

INGREDIENTS

1 large sweet potato, diced

2 tablespoons unsalted butter

1 tablespoon brown sugar

Pinch of kosher salt

Pinch of ground cinnamon

Pinch of freshly grated nutmeg

METHOD

1. Put the diced sweet potato in a jumbo mug and cover with water. Cover loosely with plastic wrap and microwave for 4 to 6 minutes until the potato is tender; Drain and set aside.

2. In a separate mug, combine the butter, sugar, salt, cinnamon, and nutmeg. Microwave for 1 to 2 minutes, stirring intermittently, until the butter and sugar have melted. Add the drained sweet potatoes, stir to coat, and serve.

> **• VARIATIONS •**
>
> **MINI MARSHMALLOWS:** After the butter has melted, stir in ¼ cup of mini marshmallows and ¼ cup pecan pieces. Cook for another 30 seconds to melt, then add the diced sweet potato.
>
> **UN-SWEET POTATOES:** Omit the sugar, cinnamon, and nutmeg, and replace them with a tablespoon each of chopped garlic, and chopped fresh rosemary. It's pretty tasty, too, with some crumbled bacon and a handful of toasted pecans.

Warm Kale with Fennel and Tangerine

MAKES 1 MUG

Kale has become the "it" vegetable, and for good reason—it's loaded with nutrients. But its flavor leans toward the bitter side. That's why I find sweeter kale recipes more enjoyable. Here, the fennel, tangerine, and honey get the job done.

INGREDIENTS

1 tablespoon olive oil

¼ cup sliced red onion

1 cup thinly sliced fennel bulb

2 cups chopped kale

Finely grated zest and juice of 1 tangerine (or orange)

1 teaspoon honey

¼ teaspoon kosher salt

¼ teaspoon freshly ground black pepper

METHOD

In a large mug, combine the oil, onion, garlic, and fennel. Microwave for 2 to 3 minutes until vegetables are tender. Add the kale, orange zest and juice, honey, salt, and pepper and toss to coat. Microwave for another 1 to 2 minutes until the kale has softened and warmed through.

Fried Green Tomatoes

MAKES 1 MUG

Historically, this dish was a way to utilize tomatoes that were otherwise inedible. Fried green tomatoes are usually fried in a skillet to create their crispy, toasted coating. This recipe is a simulation, intended to produce a similar experience. It's not the real thing, but it will fulfill your old-timey craving.

INGREDIENTS

2 tablespoons unsalted butter

¼ teaspoon kosher salt

¼ teaspoon freshly ground black pepper

¼ cup grated Parmesan cheese

2 tablespoons panko or regular bread crumbs

1 large green tomato, diced

METHOD

Put the butter in a large mug and microwave 1 to 2 minutes until melted. Add the salt, pepper, grated cheese, and bread crumbs and stir to mix. Add the diced tomato and toss to coat. Microwave for another 1 to 2 minutes until tender and warmed through. Serve immediately.

• VARIATIONS •

CORNMEAL: More often than not, fried green tomatoes are coated in cornmeal. But cornmeal doesn't soften fast enough in the microwave. You can, however, use an instant or quick-cooking corn flour in place of the bread crumbs for a similar effect.

Cauliflower Gratin

MAKES 1 MUG

I love cauliflower, but I can never use it without thinking of brains. Perhaps this is a lingering memory of my childhood—or Pee Wee Herman.

INGREDIENTS

1½ cups cauliflower, chopped into bite-size pieces

2 tablespoons unsalted butter

¼ teaspoon kosher salt

¼ teaspoon freshly ground black pepper

¼ teaspoon dried herbes de Provence or dried thyme

¼ cup grated Gruyère or Swiss-style cheese

1 tablespoon grated Parmesan cheese

METHOD

1. Put the cauliflower in a large mug and cover with water. Cover loosely with plastic wrap and microwave for 3 to 5 minutes until tender. Drain and set aside.

2. In a separate mug, combine the butter, salt, pepper, and herbs and microwave for 1 to 2 minutes, stirring intermittently, until the butter has melted. Add the drained cauliflower and stir to coat. Top with Gruyère and Parmesan cheeses and microwave for another 30 to 60 seconds until melted. Serve immediately.

Garlic Mash

A hint of garlic really spiffs up a plain old potato. When cooked whole, garlic cloves take on a lovely sweetness. If you like your garlicky essence a bit stronger, see the variations for an option using chopped garlic, which releases the garlic's stronger oils.

INGREDIENTS

1 large russet potato, diced

3 garlic cloves, minced

¼ teaspoon kosher salt

¼ teaspoon freshly ground black pepper

1 tablespoon unsalted butter

¼ cup heavy cream

METHOD

1. Put the potatoes and garlic in a large mug and cover with water. Cover loosely with plastic wrap and microwave for 5 to 8 minutes until tender. Drain and smash the potatoes and garlic with a fork.

2. Top the cooked potatoes with salt, pepper, butter, and cream. Microwave for 1 to 2 minutes, stirring and smashing intermittently with a fork, until the butter has melted. Serve immediately.

• VARIATIONS •

CHEESY: Cheese can only enhance a potato. Add ¼ cup of Jack, Havarti, muenster, or cheddar cheese. Goat, blue, cream cheese, and Brie work, too. Just avoid the stringier varieties.

VEGETABLE OPTIONS: This same dish works really well with other mashable root vegetables, including celery root and parsnip. Or try it with an interesting potato variety, like purple Peruvians.

Glazed Carrots

MAKES 1 MUG

Good glazed carrots are hard to find. They are usually made too sweet and too mushy. This version is the perfect balance of flavor and texture.

INGREDIENTS

1 large carrot, cut into rounds

2 tablespoons unsalted butter

Pinch of granulated sugar

¼ teaspoon kosher salt

¼ teaspoon freshly grated nutmeg

1 scallion

METHOD

1. Put the carrot rounds in a large mug and cover with water. Cover loosely with plastic wrap and microwave for 2 to 3 minutes until tender. Drain and set aside.

2. In a separate mug, combine the butter, sugar, salt, nutmeg, and scallion. Microwave for 1 to 2 minutes until the butter has melted. Add the drained carrots, stir to coat, and serve.

> • VARIATIONS •
>
> **GINGER CARROTS:** Add ¼ teaspoon of peeled and grated fresh ginger and a drop of sesame oil to the butter.
>
> **GARLIC CARROTS:** Add 1 clove of minced garlic to the butter mug.
>
> **CURRIED CARROTS:** Omit the nutmeg, and add, instead, 1 teaspoon of your favorite curry powder or curry paste.

Spoon Bread

This old-fashioned side dish is more of a pudding or a soufflé than a bread. Early settlers were forced to get creative with cornmeal because wheat had not yet been cultivated in the New World when they arrived. I think they had a winner with this one.

INGREDIENTS

1 cup whole milk

¼ cup cornmeal

¼ teaspoon kosher salt

1 large egg

½ teaspoon baking powder

1 tablespoon unsalted butter

¼ cup corn kernels, fresh, frozen, or drained canned

METHOD

1. In a large mug, stir together the milk, cornmeal, and salt. Microwave for 3 to 5 minutes, stirring intermittently, until the cornmeal has absorbed the liquid and thickened. Let sit at room temperature for 5 minutes to cool slightly and soften.

2. Stir in the egg, baking powder, butter, and corn. Cook for another 1 to 2 minutes until the batter is risen and firm. Serve immediately.

• VARIATIONS •

WHIP IT: Some versions of this recipe have an almost soufflé texture, which comes from whipped egg whites. To make it this way, separate your eggs. Stir in the yolk as directed, whip the white stiff and fold it in at the end.

SPICY: Corn lends itself naturally to a bit of spicy heat. Add 1 tablespoon of diced jalapeño or canned green chiles with the corn.

CHEESY: Stir in ¼ cup of grated cheddar, Jack, Swiss, or goat cheese with the corn.

Mediterranean Quinoa

MAKES 1 MUG

Quinoa (pronounced *keen-wah*) has been eaten for centuries in South America. It originated in the high Andes, and was prized for its high protein content. It was unknown to the rest of the world until recently. Now it is superchic and readily available. This recipe is not Andean in nature, but rather, takes its flavor profile from the Mediterranean. Quinoa cooks much faster than other grains, which makes it perfect for mugging.

INGREDIENTS

½ cup quinoa

¼ cup chopped red onion

1 garlic clove, minced

¼ teaspoon kosher salt

1 cup water

1 tablespoon olive oil

1 teaspoon minced fresh oregano leaves

1 teaspoon minced fresh mint leaves

Finely grated zest of ½ lemon

2 to 3 cherry tomatoes, chopped

2 tablespoons crumbled feta cheese

METHOD

1. In a large mug, combine the quinoa, onion, garlic, salt, and water and stir to combine. Cover loosely with plastic wrap and microwave for 3 to 5 minutes until the water is boiling. Set aside, covered, for 20 minutes to allow the quinoa to absorb the water. Cook another 2 to 3 minutes until tender.

2. Stir in the olive oil, oregano, mint, lemon zest, and tomatoes. Microwave for another minute to warm through. Serve immediately, topped with the feta.

• VARIATIONS •

SALTY QUINOA: Add a tablespoon of capers, olives, or chopped anchovies with the tomatoes to heighten the Mediterranean-ness.

Minted Tabbouleh

Bulgur is a quick-cooking wheat that has been cracked and partially precooked. Tabbouleh is an ancient Arab dish, but it seems almost tailor-made for microwave cooking

INGREDIENTS

½ cup bulgur wheat

1 scallion

1 garlic clove, minced

Pinch of kosher salt

1 cup water

1 tablespoon olive oil

2 tablespoons minced fresh mint leaves

Finely grated zest of ½ lemon

2 to 3 cherry tomatoes, chopped

METHOD

1. In a large mug, combine the bulgur, scallion, garlic, salt, and water and stir to combine. Cover loosely with plastic wrap and microwave for 3 to 5 minutes until the grain is tender. Set aside for 5 to 10 minutes to let the bulgur absorb the remaining water.

2. Stir in the olive oil, mint, lemon zest, and tomatoes. At this point, you can microwave it for another minute to warm through, serve it as is, or chill it. There is no wrong temperature!

> ## • VARIATIONS •
>
> **CHICKPEAS:** Turn this dish into a complete protein with the addition of ¼ cup of rinsed and drained canned garbanzo beans (aka chickpeas). Stir them in with the tomatoes.

Ratatouille

This dish was well loved way before Disney's charming rat taught it to the world. This quick version will not get you a Michelin star, but it will mentally whisk you away to Provence.

INGREDIENTS

1 tablespoon olive oil

¼ cup chopped yellow onion

1 garlic clove, minced

½ teaspoon dried herbes de Provence, or dried thyme

¼ cup seeded and diced red bell pepper

½ cup chopped zucchini

½ cup diced eggplant

½ cup diced tomato

¼ teaspoon kosher salt

¼ teaspoon freshly ground black pepper

2 tablespoons minced fresh basil leaves

2 tablespoons minced fresh flat-leaf parsley

METHOD

In a jumbo mug, combine the oil, onion, garlic, herbs, and bell peppers and microwave for 1 to 2 minutes until vegetables are tender. Add the zucchini, eggplant, tomato, salt, and black pepper and toss to combine. Microwave for another 2 to 5 minutes until the zucchini and eggplant are tender. Stir in basil and parsley and serve.

Fried Rice

This recipe was traditionally created as a way to use up leftover rice. If you don't happen to have any leftovers on hand, you can cook a your own rice in the microwave using the instructions at the top of this chapter (see page 130).

INGREDIENTS

1 teaspoon vegetable oil

½ teaspoon sesame oil

1 teaspoon soy sauce, plus more as needed

½ teaspoon peeled and grated fresh ginger

1 garlic clove, minced

1 teaspoon rice vinegar

1 cup cooked rice

¼ cup diced carrot

¼ cup peas, fresh or frozen

1 scallion

1 large egg, beaten

METHOD

1. In a large mug, combine the oils, soy sauce, ginger, and garlic. Microwave for 30 to 60 seconds until garlic is tender. Stir in the vinegar, rice, carrots, peas, and scallion and microwave for 1 to 2 minutes to warm through.

2. Flatten the top of the rice and pour the beaten egg on top. Microwave for another 1 to 2 minutes until the egg is cooked. Stir the mixture together thoroughly, and serve with additional soy sauce as needed.

• VARIATIONS •

PROTEIN RICE: It is easy to enhance this dish with pork, chicken, shrimp, or tofu. Just fold in ¼ cup of precooked meat or seafood or diced tofu with the rice.

8

mug
sweets

I happen to know that there is already a cookbook with great collection of mug desserts (because I wrote it). But if you are bored with mug cakes, this chapter will definitely rev up your after-dinner engines.

Pumpkin Cheesecake

I usually only see this dessert in the fall. But I see no reason to limit its production to that time of year.

INGREDIENTS

½ cup crumbled gingersnaps or graham crackers

1 tablespoon unsalted butter

8 ounces cream cheese, softened

⅛ cup packed brown sugar

Pinch of kosher salt

⅛ teaspoon pumpkin pie spice (or a pinch each of cinnamon, nutmeg, ginger, and a tiny pinch of clove)

¼ cup pumpkin puree

1 large egg

Whipped cream or sour cream, for serving

METHOD

1. Divide the gingersnaps between two large mugs. Top each with half of the butter. Microwave separately for 20 to 30 seconds each until the butter has melted. Stir the crumbs so that they are well coated with the butter. Set aside.

2. In a jumbo mug or bowl, beat the cream cheese, sugar, and salt together with a fork until creamy and lump-free. Add the pie spice, pumpkin puree, and egg and beat until smooth. Divide the cheese filling between the two mugs, plopping the batter on top of the crumbs, and giving each mug a little tap to settle the filling into the crumbs. Microwave separately for 1½ to 2½ minutes each until the filling is slightly puffed. Chill completely, and serve with a dollop of whipped cream or sour cream.

Crème Brûlée

MAKES 1 MUG

Crème brûlée is nothing but a basic vanilla custard. It is its finishing touch—the caramelized top—that gets everyone all excited. The best way to accomplish this is with a butane or propane torch, but a toaster oven will do in a pinch. For the top, I prefer to use turbinado sugar (aka "Sugar in the Raw") because it is harder to burn, makes a thicker crust, and a richer flavor. But, in its absence, white sugar works, too.

INGREDIENTS

½ cup heavy cream (Flavor can be added here by steeping ingredients such as coffee, tea, spices, herbs, or citrus zest for 10 minutes, then straining.)

1 large egg yolk

2 tablespoons granulated sugar

¼ vanilla bean, scraped, or ½ teaspoon pure vanilla extract

1 to 2 tablespoons turbinado sugar (Sugar in the Raw), or granulated sugar

METHOD

1. Combine the egg yolk, granulated sugar, and vanilla in a large mug and whisk together thoroughly. Set aside.

2. Pour the cream into a large mug and microwave for 1 to 1½ minutes until very hot. Drizzle the hot cream slowly into egg mug while whisking with a fork. Place the mug in a slightly larger microwaveable container (like a cereal bowl). Fill the bowl with water to create a water bath for your mug. Microwave the custard for 30 to 60 seconds until set. Remove from the microwave and the water bath, let cool to room temperature, then chill for at least 30 minutes.

3. To caramelize the top, sprinkle the turbinado sugar on top of the chilled custard, and slowly burn the top with a blowtorch, moving the flame back and forth continuously, so that the melting is done evenly. If you are using a toaster oven, use the broil setting, and heat until melted and golden. (The time it takes to caramelize fully will probably overcook your custard using this method).

Apple Brown Betty

This quick version of fruit crisp uses crumbs rather than streusel. It's a great way to utilize stale bread, broken cookies, or the last donut.

INGREDIENTS

2 tablespoons unsalted butter

1 large apple, peeled, cored, and diced (you can use a variety of fruit here, including pears, berries, or stone fruits)

1 tablespoon brown sugar

Pinch of cinnamon

Pinch of freshly grated nutmeg

Pinch of kosher salt

1 tablespoon granulated sugar

¼ cup bread or cracker crumbs

1 tablespoon old-fashioned rolled oats

1 tablespoon chopped pecans or walnuts

Vanilla ice cream, or whipped cream, for serving

METHOD

1. In a large mug, combine 1 tablespoon of the butter with the apples. Microwave for 2 to 3 minutes until the fruit is tender. Stir in the brown sugar, cinnamon, nutmeg, salt, and set aside.

2. Put the remaining 1 tablespoon butter and the granulated sugar in a separate mug, and microwave for 30 to 60 seconds until melted. Add the crumbs, oats, and nuts and mix thoroughly. Sprinkle this mixture on top of the apples. Microwave for another 30 to 60 seconds to warm through. Serve with a scoop of vanilla ice cream or a dollop of whipped cream.

• VARIATIONS •

ROSEMARY-APPLE: This is my all-time favorite apple combination. Add 1 teaspoon finely minced fresh rosemary with the apples as they cook. You'll be glad you did.

APPLE CHEDDAR: Serve a twist on the old-timer's favorite, apple pie with cheddar cheese. Before you top the cooked apples with the crumbs, sprinkle on 2 tablespoons of grated cheddar cheese.

Blackberry Crisp

Crisp topping (aka streusel) is also a common element of breakfast baking. (You'll find it in this book's recipes for muffins and coffee cake.) In fact, it is part of a pastry chef's pantry staples. Take a hint from the pastry chefs and keep a container of it in your freezer. Then you'll be crisp-ready.

INGREDIENTS

Streusel Topping

½ cup whole wheat or all-purpose flour

2 tablespoons brown sugar

2 tablespoons unsalted butter, cubed and chilled

Filling

2 cups fresh or frozen blackberries

1 tablespoon granulated sugar

Pinch of kosher salt

¼ teaspoon freshly grated nutmeg

½ teaspoon cornstarch

Vanilla ice cream or whipped cream, for serving

METHOD

1. *To make the topping:* In a large mug, mix together the flour and brown sugar. Add the chilled butter and cut it in, using a fork, until the mixture resembles coarse crumbs. Set aside in the fridge.

2. *To make the filling:* In a second mug, combine the berries, granulated sugar, salt, nutmeg, and cornstarch. Toss so that the berries are well coated. Pour the crumb mixture on top of the fruit and microwave for 2 to 3 minutes until the fruit is bubbly. Serve warm with a scoop of vanilla ice cream or a dollop of whipped cream.

> **• VARIATIONS •**
>
> **FRUIT OPTIONS:** Try the same method with any ripe fruit. It's perfect with peaches, pears, and berries. If your crisp fruit is a bit tarter, like rhubarb, sour cherries, or cranberries, add another 2 tablespoons of sugar, for a total of ¼ cup. Sugar amounts may need adjustment, as the natural variation of sweetness varies a lot in fruit.

Butterscotch Pudding

MAKES 1 MUG

Pudding is easy and quick to make in the microwave, but true enjoyment comes only after the pudding has chilled. This is the sad truth of custards. So plan ahead.

INGREDIENTS

2 teaspoons unsalted butter

1 teaspoon pure vanilla extract

1 teaspoon Scotch whiskey

1 tablespoon cornstarch

2 tablespoons brown sugar

1 cup whole milk

1 large egg

Whipped cream, for serving

METHOD

1. Put the butter, vanilla, and Scotch in a large mug. Cover loosely with plastic wrap and microwave for 30 to 60 seconds until the butter has melted and started to brown. Set aside.

2. In a second mug, stir together the cornstarch and brown sugar. Slowly stir in the cold milk, and whisk to combine. Microwave for 3 to 5 minutes, stirring intermittently (about every minute), until the mixture has thickened.

3. Stir the butter mixture into the thickened milk. Crack the egg into the emptied butter mug, and whisk it with a fork until frothy. Beat half of the hot, thickened milk into the egg, then slowly stir in the rest. Microwave for another 1 to 2 minutes until the pudding just begins to bubble and thicken. Cover with plastic wrap and chill to set. Serve with a dollop of whipped cream.

• VARIATION •

CHOCOLATE PUDDING: Omit the Scotch. Combine the milk with ¼ cup chocolate chips and microwave for 1 to 2 minutes. Then proceed with the recipe as written.

Fudge Brownie

Once you see how easy this is, every night will be brownie night—or every morning, or every afternoon. You get the idea.

INGREDIENTS

2 tablespoons unsalted butter

¼ cup dark chocolate chips (semisweet or bittersweet)

1 large egg

¼ cup sugar

3 tablespoons sour cream

¼ teaspoon pure vanilla extract

Pinch of kosher salt

2 tablespoons unsweetened cocoa powder

2 tablespoons all-purpose flour

Confectioners' sugar, vanilla ice cream, or fresh berries, for serving

METHOD

Combine the butter and chocolate chips in a large mug and microwave for 30 to 60 seconds until melted. Whisk in the egg with a fork. Add the granulated sugar, sour cream, vanilla, and salt. Stir in the cocoa powder and flour and beat until smooth. Divide the batter between two mugs and microwave for 1½ to 2½ minutes each until risen and firm. Serve immediately, topped with confectioners' sugar, vanilla ice cream, or fresh berries.

• VARIATIONS •

MEXICAN CHOCOLATE: Replace the chocolate chips with chopped Ibarra chocolate (designed for Mexican hot chocolate), or add a pinch of cinnamon to the recipe above.

WHITE CHOCOLATE: Replace the chocolate chips with white chocolate chips. These typically melt faster, so adjust the cook time accordingly.

NUTS: Add up to ¼ cup of your favorite chopped nuts with the cocoa and flour.

Indian Pudding

This American colonial classic gets its name from the cornmeal, which was first known as "Indian meal." Wheat flour was unavailable to early settlers, but they managed to create this creamy rich pudding without it.

INGREDIENTS

¼ cup cornmeal

¼ cup half-and-half

½ cup whole milk

¼ cup granulated sugar

2 tablespoons molasses

Pinch of ground cinnamon

Pinch of freshly grated nutmeg

Pinch of ground ginger

Pinch of ground cloves

Pinch of kosher salt

¼ cup heavy cream

Whipped cream and rum-soaked raisins, for serving

METHOD

1. Combine the cornmeal and half-and-half in a large mug and microwave for 30 to 60 seconds to warm through. Set aside.

2. In a separate mug, combine the milk, sugar, and molasses. Microwave for 1 to 2 minutes, stirring intermittently, until the milk is very hot and the sugar has dissolved. Slowly whisk the milk into the cornmeal mixture. Add the spices, salt, and cream and mix thoroughly. Microwave in 30-second increments until the mixture just begins to bubble and looks set. Chill the pudding for 30 minutes to set completely. Serve with a dollop of whipped cream and a tablespoon of raisins that have been plumped in rum. (Soak them overnight, or warm and steep for 30 minutes.)

Peanut Brittle

MAKES ABOUT 2 CUPS OF SHATTERED BRITTLE

This recipe is dangerous. And not just because you'll find yourself making it way more than you should. Caramelized sugar is scalding hot, so be sure to have your oven mitts at the ready.

INGREDIENTS

¼ cup sugar

2 tablespoons corn syrup

¼ cup dry roasted and salted peanuts (you can also try this with other nuts, such as almonds, pistachios, cashews, or pecans)

1 teaspoon unsalted butter

½ teaspoon pure vanilla extract

¼ teaspoon baking soda

METHOD

1. Combine the sugar and corn syrup in a jumbo mug and microwave for 3 to 5 minutes until the mixture is very hot and bubbly and turns a light amber color. Add the peanuts and continue to cook in 30-second increments until the mixture is brown. (Be careful, because it can easily go too long, and burn. I look for the first indications of smoke to determine doneness.)

2. Place a large sheet of wax or parchment paper on the countertop, and coat it lightly with no-stick spray. Stir the butter, vanilla, and baking soda into the sugar mixture and mix until foamy. Carefully pour the mixture out onto the prepared paper, and spread smooth. Allow to cool, then break apart into bite-size pieces.

• VARIATIONS •

SPICY: Sweet and heat make for some great snacking. Add a pinch of cayenne pepper or hot red chile flakes with the baking soda.

ORANGE ZEST: Add a teaspoon of finely grated orange zest with the baking soda for a bright, citrus punch.

Rhubarb Cobbler

This recipe can easily be reinterpreted as a "crisp" or "crumble" by replacing the biscuit top with ¼ cup of streusel. You'll find that recipe on page 159.

INGREDIENTS

Cobbler Topping

½ cup all-purpose flour

¼ teaspoon baking powder

1 tablespoon granulated sugar

Pinch of freshly grated nutmeg

Pinch of kosher salt

3 tablespoons unsalted butter, chilled

2 tablespoons buttermilk (or regular milk)

Filling

1½ cups diced fresh rhubarb

3 tablespoons brown sugar

1 tablespoon honey

1 teaspoon all-purpose flour

Pinch of ground cinnamon

Pinch of kosher salt

Confectioners' sugar or whipped cream, for serving

METHOD

1. To make the cobbler topping: In a jumbo mug, combine the flour, baking powder, sugar, nutmeg, and salt and mix well. Add the butter and cut it in with a fork until the mixture resembles coarse crumbs. Stir in the buttermilk just until combined. Set the cobbler topping aside.

2. To make the filling: In a second large mug, combine the rhubarb, brown sugar, and honey. Add the flour, cinnamon, and salt and toss to coat the rhubarb. Microwave for 2 to 3 minutes until the rhubarb has softened. Scoop the topping on top of the rhubarb, then microwave for another 1½ to 2½ minutes until risen and firm. Serve immediately topped with confectioners' sugar or whipped cream.

> **• VARIATIONS •**
>
> **FRUIT OPTIONS:** Any fresh fruit makes a good cobbler. Experiment with the seasons. You may need to adjust the first cooking time, as rhubarb takes longer to cook than berries or stone fruits.

Spanish Flan

MAKES 1 MUG

Flan is a vanilla custard baked with caramel on the bottom, which becomes a sauce when the finished custard is inverted onto a plate. The European version uses milk, and is lighter than the Latin American version, which uses condensed milk.

INGREDIENTS

Custard

1 cup whole milk

¼ cup granulated sugar

¼ vanilla bean, scraped, or ½ teaspoon pure vanilla extract

1 large egg

Caramel

1 tablespoon sugar

1 tablespoon water

METHOD

1. *To make the custard:* Put the milk, sugar, and vanilla in a large mug and microwave for 1 to 2 minutes until the milk is hot and the sugar has dissolved.

2. In a second mug, whisk the egg with a fork until frothy. Slowly drizzle in the milk while whisking. Microwave the custard in 30-second increments until the custard sets and barely begins to bubble. Cool at room temperature, then refrigerate for at least 30 minutes. (If you can plan ahead, chilling for several hours is always better for custards.)

3. *Just before serving, make the caramel:* Combine the sugar and water in a mug and microwave in 30-second increments until caramelized. (This usually takes about 1½ minutes). Be careful not to overcook; sugar burns quickly in a microwave. Pour the caramel over the chilled custard and serve.

Peanut Butter S'Mores

MAKES 1 MUG

My Girl Scouts became proficient in microwave s'mores the year we were hit by El Niño. It was then that they came up with this variation of the original. There is no better way to run a rainy day meeting of fidgety girls than to get them all hopped up on sugar. Just be sure to hide the glue guns.

INGREDIENTS

1 tablespoon peanut butter

¼ cup chocolate chips

¼ cup mini marshmallows

2 graham crackers, broken into bite-size pieces

METHOD

Combine the peanut butter and chocolate chips in a large mug and stir together. Add the mini marshmallows and graham cracker bits and toss to evenly distribute. Microwave for 30 to 60 seconds until the chocolate and marshmallows have melted. Cool slightly, and serve.

• VARIATIONS •

OREOS: If you replace the graham crackers with crumbled Oreos, you will be a hero.

CHOCOLATE OPTIONS: Hershey's bars are the standard s'more ingredient, but chocolate chips are more mug-friendly. That said, no one would turn up their nose at a s'more made with broken bits of candy bar. Instead of a Hershey's bar, try a Kit Kat, a peanut butter cup, or even a Snickers. (This is a great way to use up those leftover Halloween candy minis.)

Snickerdoodles

From what I have been told, Snickerdoodle is an old American folk hero. He drives a peanut car, and saves the day with the help of his uncle, Yankee, and his cousin Polly Wolly. It's an old-timey story for an old-timey recipe.

INGREDIENTS

1 tablespoon unsalted butter

2 tablespoons granulated sugar

Pinch of kosher salt

¼ teaspoon pure vanilla extract

¼ teaspoon ground cinnamon

1 large egg yolk

3 tablespoons self-rising flour (or use all-purpose flour plus ¼ teaspoon baking powder)

METHOD

1. Put the butter in a large mug and microwave for 30 to 60 seconds until melted. Stir in the sugar, salt, vanilla, cinnamon, and egg yolk. Add the flour, and beat until well combined. Microwave for 2 to 3 minutes until risen and firm. Serve warm with another mug filled with milk.

> **• VARIATIONS •**
>
> **COOKIE-SIZE:** Make these more cookielike by microwaving a tablespoon of batter at a time, for 30 to 60 seconds each, plopping them out onto a plate, and dusting with confectioners' sugar.

Pecan Pie

The crumbled vanilla wafers in this recipe serve to simulate a pie crust. If you want to make a legit pie, place a precooked pie crust (homemade or store-bought) in a glass or ceramic pie pan, then quadruple this recipe and cook them together in the microwave.

INGREDIENTS

1 tablespoon unsalted butter

1 large egg

¼ cup dark corn syrup

2 teaspoons brown sugar

1 teaspoon all-purpose flour

⅛ teaspoon pure vanilla extract

¼ cup pecan pieces

3 to 4 crumbled vanilla wafers or graham crackers

Whipped cream, for serving

METHOD

Put the butter in a large mug and microwave for 30 to 60 seconds until melted. Add the egg and beat with a fork until frothy. Stir in the corn syrup, brown sugar, flour, and vanilla and mix thoroughly. Fold in the pecans, and top with the crumbled wafers. Microwave for 1 to 2 minutes until risen and firm; the top should look dry. Cool completely at room temperature, then chill for at least 30 minutes in the fridge; this dessert is best when cold. Serve with a dollop of whipped cream.

Chocolate Chip Cookie

When you have a cookie craving, there is really only one recipe you want. This will make two mugs of cookie, but we all know finishing off one giant mug cookie is no big deal.

INGREDIENTS

3 tablespoons unsalted butter, softened

2 tablespoons granulated sugar

2 tablespoons brown sugar

Pinch of kosher salt

1 large egg

½ teaspoon pure vanilla extract

½ cup self-rising flour (or ½ cup of all-purpose flour and ⅛ teaspoon baking powder)

¼ cup chocolate chips (semisweet or bittersweet)

METHOD

1. In a large mug, combine the butter and sugars. Mix thoroughly with a fork. Stir in the salt, egg, and vanilla. Add the flour, a little at a time, and beat the batter until smooth. Fold in the chocolate chips.

2. Divide the batter between two mugs and microwave each separately for 1 to 2 minutes until risen and firm. Cool slightly before serving.

> **• VARIATIONS •**
>
> **GARNISHES GALORE:** You can add anything you like to this recipe—nuts, butterscotch chips, spices, coconut, raisins, sunflower seeds, M&M's, Skittles— you name it. Keep the added garnish to about ½ cup.

Common Food Substitutions

Baking Powder: 1 teaspoon, can be replaced by ¼ teaspoon baking soda + ⅝ teaspoon cream of tartar, or ¼ teaspoon baking soda + ½ cup buttermilk

Broth/Stock: 1 cup can be replaced by 1 bouillon cube or 1 teaspoon granulated bouillon mixed with 1 cup boiling water

Butter: 1 cup can be replaced by an equal amount of margarine, or ¾ cup vegetable oil, lard, or shortening

Buttermilk: 1 cup, can be replaced by 1 cup yogurt, or 1 cup milk + 1 tablespoon lemon juice, or 1 cup milk + 1 tablespoon vinegar, or 1 cup milk + 1 teaspoon cream of tartar

Chocolate: Semisweet can be made by adding 1 tablespoon of sugar for every ½ ounce of unsweetened chocolate

Cornstarch: 1 tablespoon, can be replaced by 2 tablespoons all-purpose flour

Corn syrup: 1 cup, can be replaced by 1¼ cup sugar + ¼ cup water

Cream: 1 cup, can be replaced by ¾ cup whole milk + ⅓ cup butter

Egg: 1 whole, can be replaced by 2 yolks, or 2 whites, or 3½ tablespoons egg substitute

Egg white: 1, can be replaced by 1 tablespoon powdered egg white, or 2 tablespoons frozen egg whites

Egg yolk: 1, can be replaced by 2 tablespoons powdered yolk, or 3½ teaspoons frozen yolk

Flour: When used as a thickener, 1 tablespoon of flour can be replaced with 1½ teaspoons cornstarch or potato starch, or 2 teaspoons arrowroot

Cake Flour: 1 cup, can be replaced by 1 cup all-purpose flour + 1 tablespoon cornstarch

Garlic: 1 clove can be replaced with ⅛ teaspoon garlic powder

Honey: 1 cup, can be replaced by 1¼ cups white sugar, and increase recipe liquid by ¼ cup

Lemon juice: This can be replaced with half as much white wine vinegar (for savory applications) or cider vinegar (for sweet applications)

Milk: 1 cup, can be replaced by ½ cup evaporated milk + ½ cup water, or ¼ cup powdered milk + ⅔ cup water

Conversion Tables and Substitutions

CONVERSION TABLES		MEASUREMENT EQUIVALENTS				
1½ teaspoons	=	½ tablespoon	=	¼ fluid ounce		
3 teaspoons	=	1 tablespoon	=	½ fluid ounce		
1 tablespoon	=	3 teaspoons	=	½ fluid ounce		
2 tablespoons	=	⅛ cup	=	1 fluid ounce		
4 tablespoons	=	¼ cup	=	2 fluid ounces		
8 tablespoons	=	½ cup	=	4 fluid ounces		
12 tablespoons	=	¾ cup	=	6 fluid ounces		
16 tablespoons	=	1 cup	=	8 fluid ounces		
1 cup	=	16 tablespoons	=	8 fluid ounces		
2 cups	=	1 pint	=	16 fluid ounces		
4 cups	=	2 pint	=	32 fluid ounces	=	1 quart
16 cups	=	4 quart	=	128 fluid ounces	=	1 gallon

TEMPERATURE

To convert Fahrenheit to Celsius, subtract 32, divide by 9, multiply by 5.

To convert Celsius to Fahrenheit, divide by 5, multiply by 9, add 32.

FAHRENHEIT	CELSIUS		FAHRENHEIT	CELSIUS
32°F	0°C (Freezing)		250°F	121°C (Hard Ball)
50°F	10°C		270°F	132°C (Soft Crack)
100°F	37.8°C		300°F	149° (Hard Crack)
120°F	48.9°C		320°F	160°C (Caramel)
150°F	65.6°C		350°F	177°C
200°F	93.3°C		400°F	205°C
212°F	100°C (Boiling)		450°F	233°C
240°F	115°C (Soft Ball)		500°F	260°C

WEIGHT

To convert ounces to grams, multiply by 28.35

To convert grams into ounces, multiply by 0.03527

To convert kilograms into pounds, multiply by 2.2046

When multiplying large weight, round to nearest whole number

US	METRIC (APPROXIMATE)	US	METRIC (APPROXIMATE)
1/2 ounce	15 grams	8 ounces (1/2 pound)	225 grams
2/3 ounce	20 grams	12 ounces	340 grams
3/4 ounce	22 grams	16 ounces (1 pound)	455 grams
1 ounce	30 grams	2 pounds	910 grams
2 ounces	55 grams	3 pounds	1 kilogram,365 grams
4 ounces (1/4 pound)	115 grams	4 pounds	1 kilogram,820 grams
5 ounces	140 grams	5 pounds	2 kilogram,275 grams

VOLUME

To convert milliliters into ounces, multiply by 0.0338

To convert milliliters into pints, multiply by 0.0021125

To convert liters into ounces, multiply by 33.8

To convert liters into pints, multiply by 2.1125

To convert liters into quarts, multiply by 1.05625

To convert quarts into liters, multiply by 0.946

When multiplying large volume, round to nearest whole number

US	METRIC (APPROXIMATE)	US	METRIC (APPROXIMATE)
1/2 teaspoon	2.5 milliliters	1 cup	237 milliliters
1 teaspoon	5 milliliter	1 pint	475 milliliters
1 tablespoon	15 milliliters	1 quart	950 milliliters

LENGTH

To convert inches into centimeters, multiply by 2.54

To convert centimeters into inches, multiply by 0.3937

To convert meters into inches, multiply by 39.3701

Index